Penguin Books

BUSINESS WARGAMES

Dr Barrie G. James has spent many years in the health care industry with particular responsibilities in business development, internal marketing consultancy and strategic planning. He has extensive experience of business operations in the Americas, Europe, Japan, the Middle East and Africa.

Among his many other achievements he has successfully marketed a wide variety of products in a diversity of markets; from research concepts in biotechnology and human and animal health pharmaceuticals throughout the world, to suntan products in Scandinavia, denture cleaners in Canada, hair straighteners in Africa, welding supplies in the U.K., and cough and cold products in the Middle East.

He holds a Masters degree and Ph.D. in Management from Brunel University and has contributed many articles to books and magazines on business and marketing strategy. He was awarded the McKinsey prize for the best business article published in the United Kingdom in 1972 and his two previous books have become standard business texts in their area.

Dr James is currently Head of Marketing Development for a major pharmaceutical company.

Barrie G. James

BUSINESS WARGAMES

Penguin Books

Penguin Books Ltd, Harmondsworth, Middlesex, England
Viking Penguin Inc., 40 West 23rd Street, New York, New York 10010, U.S.A.
Penguin Books Australia Ltd, Ringwood, Victoria, Australia
Penguin Books Canada Ltd, 2801 John Street, Markham, Ontario, Canada L3R 1B4
Penguin Books (N.Z.) Ltd, 182–190 Wairau Road, Auckland 10, New Zealand

First published by Abacus Press 1984
Published in Penguin Books 1985

Copyright Abacus Press, 1984
All rights reserved

Made and printed in Great Britain by
Richard Clay (The Chaucer Press) Ltd, Bungay, Suffolk
Typeset in Times

For Honey James (1967–83)

CONTENTS

FOREWORD

This is one of those books which one feels should have been written before. After all, defence and business are two of the major preoccupations of mankind. The huge budgets which governments invest in armaments and armies are similar to the funds committed in research and development, production and marketing, by multinational corporations. The problems of leadership, communication and logistics across continents in times of war are comparable in size and complexity with the difficulties of managing a large international business such as Ford, Shell or Unilever.

Any businessman who has served in the armed forces, or who has an interest in military history, is struck at one time or another by the similarities, and the differences, between war and business. Business literature is full of military terms. We talk of 'price wars', 'advertising campaigns', 'battles for market share', and so on. And of course, the notions of business strategy and strategic planning come from the military idea of strategy as opposed to tactics.

In this book Barrie James has set out to do what many of us would like to do for ourselves. He has made a detailed comparison of current thinking and practice on military strategy and business strategy.

The book is ambitious. Business strategy and military strategy are each substantial studies in themselves. To compare the two requires a thorough knowledge of both. It is also a pioneering effort. Whilst military strategy has been studied and analysed for many centuries, business strategy as a field of study is less than a generation old and it is only in recent years that techniques have been developed for strategic analysis.

The book has three potential markets. Businessmen — particularly those interested in strategy — will find here a collection of valuable insights into business strategy, and over a hundred brief case histories illustrating the critical factors for success or failure in today's markets. Most of the illustrations are taken from business in the late 1970s and early 1980s. The second market — and a subsidiary one — would be students and readers of military strategy. Here, for the first time, army officers and military historians have an opportunity to discover what (if anything) they can learn from the study and practice of business strategy. The third market for the book is among teachers, students and researchers of business strategy. To these readers the book offers a new framework of concepts taken from the military tradition and applied to business — and an invitation to take the comparison between business and war still further.

What then emerges from this comparison between war and business?

1. It is clear that we cannot take the analogy too far. The aim of war is normally to defend or conquer land, whereas business is about controlling markets. War is waged by governments while businesses are usually private enterprises. Wars tend to be a temporary phenomenon — these days they may last only a few weeks — but large businesses sometimes operate in the same market for several generations.

    Furthermore, wars are fought in an atmosphere of crisis which produces special problems but also some advantages for the leadership. In business there are also crises, but generally the major concern is how to achieve continual improvements in productivity, product quality and customer service over long periods of time when often there is no immediate danger to the firm's survival.

2. I think Barrie James' contribution is most interesting when he analyses competition for markets. Here the competitor takes the place of the enemy and the 'battle' is for the customer purchase. Once this is conceded, the War Game translates fairly readily into the Business Game.

    Alliances or 'co-operative agreements' turn out to be important in business just as they are in war. The chapter on alliances is particularly valuable in interpreting the present business situation, for example in the automobile industry where European producers are entering into numerous joint ventures and joint supply agreements in order to try to compete with the US and Japanese companies. In analyzing the contribution of new technology, the benefits and the limitations of armaments in war translate fairly readily into the role of new products and new processes in business. Also, the impact of modern information and telecommunications technology in, say, the Falklands War, has clear implications for communication in international business. One area — logistics — is revealed as crucial to success in war but generally *neglected* in business strategy except in the case of airlines, oil companies, and some food companies where it is sometimes the focus of top management attention.

3. For the business reader in many ways 'the medium is the message'. Every maxim of war or principle of strategy is analysed in business terms with numerous examples showing the successes and the failures. In the process the reader is taken on a Cook's Tour of world business...

    US companies:— Boeing, General Motors, IBM, Texas Instruments, McDonalds, Caterpillar, DuPont, RCA, Kaman, Gillette, Philip Morris, American Hospital Supply and American Express.

    UK and European companies:— Sinclair Research, Racal, EMI, ICL, Pilkington, Philips, Heineken, Michelin, Renault, Aerospatiale, Scandinavian Airlines, Grundig, AEG-Telefunken, BMW, Hoffmann–La Roche, Nestle, and Bang & Olufsen.

    Japanese companies:— Nissan, Honda, Canon, Ricoh, Toyota, Hitachi, Fujitsu, Yamaha and Komatsu.

Many books on business are boring. Business is often presented as a mixture of economics and accounting. Barrie James comes from a different tradition — from Peter Drucker's school of entrepreneurship. To him business is about new technologies, competing for markets, and satisfying customers through technological and market innovation. Dr. James writes fluently and his enthusiasm comes through. The business reader in particular will find *Business Wargames* enjoyable and thought provoking.

Bernard Taylor

ACKNOWLEDGEMENTS

Business Wargames took a considerable time to research and write due to the complexity of the subject and the pressures of other activities. However, the book became a reality only as a result of the considerable help and support that I have received from others.

Although the idea germinated in the early 1970s, the research started after Bernard Taylor at the Administrative Staff College suggested that I make a comparison between business and military strategy in mid-1981. Colleagues and associates — Barry Wald at Syntex and Jean Chabre, Tom Gaspar, Georges Hibon and Marcel Zagamy at Merck & Co. — played a central part in formulating my early ideas for the research. I was extremely fortunate in having an avid military historian, Guy Di Carlo, as a close friend. Guy placed his extensive library at my disposal and, together with Michael Lindeman, acted as a sounding board for the original concepts.

I was able to obtain expert military advice from John Pimlott at the Royal Military Academy who provided me with the input to correct the inaccuracies which crept into the text, and with additional ideas on deterrent strategies. Steven Badsey at the Imperial War Museum steered me in a number of new directions, opening up new areas in the research, and the librarians at the Imperial War Museum in London and the International Management Institute in Geneva kindly provided me with extensive assistance in my military and business research.

Bernard Taylor proved to be a continuing source of ideas and suggestions which made the final text more concise and readable and helped me to avoid the pitfalls of moving off at tangents. Bernard was also kind enough to write the Foreword to the book. Fritz Gottschalk, an old friend and senior partner in the design consultancy Gottschalk & Ash, took the book in hand and designed the superb cover. Andrea Dittrich, Lyn Douglas and my wife Mary managed to decipher my writing and produce the typescript with good humour, despite the many revisions , and Bahman Karbassioun and Richard Pettigrew kindly provided logistical support.

My thanks are also due to my editor, Paul Harris at Abacus Press, who not only guided me successfully through the minefields of publishing in record time but also contributed the excellent illustrations which appear in *Business Wargames*.

A debt of gratitude is also due to past colleagues — notably David Bromley–Challenor, Jewell Brisick, Bob Ley, Ted Pfeffer, George Denes and Bill Helfand — who have taught me much about warfare in the market–place, and to Peter Moore–Robinson who gave me continual support during some difficult times.

Last, but not least, I owe my thanks to my long–suffering wife, Mary. Mary's enthusiasm and encouragement for *Business Wargames* provided me with the support necessary to conduct the research and write the book. Without Mary's patience and help the book could not have been written.

To you all my sincere thanks.

Since I have no pretentions that I am a military historian, I have taken as much time over the military examples as the business examples. However, it is inevitable that there will be errors and omissions for which I am completely at fault.

Barrie G. James
October 1983
Geneva

INTRODUCTION

> 'War is an art, proficiency in which depends more on experience than on study, and more on natural aptitude and judgement than on either'.
>
> David Lloyd George (1937)

This is *not* another book on a new technique for strategic analysis. *Business Wargames* is a back-to-basics approach to business strategy for the executive in the trenches of market warfare, and is about using the principles of military strategy to win battles in the market-place.

During the 1960s and 1970s business strategy became a glamorous and profitable activity. Strategic planning was a way station for the upwardly mobile executive, and strategy became a goldmine for the consulting boutiques who peddled a set of easy-to-understand but difficult-to-apply techniques, complete with their own terminology — a sort of 'stratspeak'. In the 1980s the deficiencies began to show up. Business conditions changed and the effects of the world-wide recession progressively created high levels of inflation, interest rates and unemployment which in turn created social changes in attitudes, behaviour, demographics, life-styles and values. Growth was replaced by stagnation and whole industries decayed through declines in industrial demand, the lack of cash to reinvest and the inability of consumers to purchase. Companies were forced towards retrenchment strategies rather than accelerated growth. Strategic concepts and techniques linked to growth were incapable of coping with the shift in emphasis to survival in declining and mature markets. This was compounded by the misinterpretation and misapplication of the strategic concepts which often became an end in themselves, rather than a means to an end. Strategists and management were guilty of viewing the concepts and techniques as more than analytical tools which, in reality, offered little if anything to the arguably more important strategic activities of preparation and execution. Strategists and management became mesmerized by the clinical precision and the mythology surrounding the successes of the concepts and techniques in the 1960s and 1970s and allowed strategy to move away from the battleground of the market–place to the safety of the command bunker. As a result of this preoccupation with analytical technique, strategy turned into an intellectual shell game and in the process lost touch with reality, obscuring the fundamental rule that battles for market share are won in the market–place and not in the strategists' office.

Companies fail in the market–place because their strategies are ill–conceived, poorly prepared and badly executed in relation to those of their competitors. All companies, whether large, sophisticated, or using high technology, can eventually be outmanœuvred in the market–place. Examples of this are General Motors — the world's largest manufacturing company, who failed to combat the Japanese incursions into the US automobile market; Texas Instruments' failure to market home computers as successfully as they had semiconductors; and EMI's mid–term failure with the revolutionary CAT scanner. No company is immune from making errors in strategy and companies, like old soldiers, do not keep riding into the sunset — they die if those errors in strategy are of a significant magnitude. Companies, unfortunately, tend to use the Kamikazi approach to combat in the market–place which fails just as readily as it failed against the US 5th Fleet in the battle of Okinawa, and is nothing more than a one–way business suicide mission. Tragically, companies, in addition to making errors in strategy commission, by selecting traditional and institutionalized approaches, also make errors of strategy ommission; that is, avoiding making the strategic choice. Few companies really want to fight it out with a competitor in the market–place and most attempt to avoid physical confrontation. This aversion to risk conceals another fundamental rule — if you don't fight, you can't win and if you can't win, you lose.

It is unlikely in the foreseeable future that the world will return to a period of sustained non–inflationary growth, and companies must therefore face the fact that survival and growth is now largely dependent on taking markets away from competitors, protecting business from competitive aggression, and deterring an assault on their markets. Business has always been competitive, but now more than ever companies require strategies which truly reflect the combative nature of the market–place. The closest analogy to current market conditions is war. Despite differences in degree and in kind between business and military conflict, there are remarkable similarities between the two sets of precepts. Companies and armies share common strategic manœuvres in terms of deterrence, offence, defence and alliance. They are similar in the way in which they are organized and structured. They use equivalent systems and procedures and rely on the same functions — intelligence, weaponry, logistics and communications — to provide a combat edge. The resemblance between the two forms of conflict is not surprising since both companies and armies are organisationally designed for one purpose — to fight, whether in the market or on the battlefield.

Business Wargames has been written with two aims. First, to provide the executive with a concise reading of the wide range of strategic manœuvres available to any company using the principles of military strategy; and to encourage creativity and a broadening of the approach to strategy selection as a means to break out of the inflexible, institutionalized, analytical approaches to strategy used by many companies. Secondly, to identify the common failures to appreciate the realities of market combat, and to question the heavy reliance on oversimplified formulae and complex simulation that have been adopted in the mistaken belief that the executive can plan, model and simulate his way to victory rather than fight it out in the market-place. *Business Wargames* will not prevent failure in the market-place any more than a thorough grasp of military strategy can avert defeat on the battlefield since there are no fail-safe methods of winning in either type of conflict. *Business Wargames* illustrates the success of companies which have used strategies truly emphasizing combat, and the failures of companies which have ignored the fundamental rule that battles are not won by formula and computer; they are won by the practical hands-on experience of an individual able to make the intuitively right decision at the right place and the right time.

The message of this book is simple. To survive you have to learn to fight by the rules of the game. The rules of the business game have changed in response to economic, technological and social dislocation and require a new approach to market combat. The companies that will survive and prosper in the 1980s and beyond will be those which recognize the new rules of the market-place and adopt end-game strategies which reflect the combative nature of the market–place. Those companies which continue to use game plans which are not conflict orientated will have a less–than–even chance of survival.

chapter one
THE BUSINESS WARGAME

'War is basically a conflict of wills.'

Air Marshal Sir John Slessor (1945)

Business is simply about winning battles in the market-place by outmanœuvring an opponent to obtain a superior profit position.

The following examples of business success and failure have a common denominator:

In 1951, the Univac division of Remington-Rand introduced the first commercial mainframe computer which was a technical tour de force. IBM's computers which followed in 1952 were not so impressive technically. IBM, in a successful frontal attack on Univac, used an array of weapons new to the market — a highly trained service organization, application specialists to develop computer usage, and leasing arrangements to reduce customer capital investment. By 1956, IBM had taken leadership with an 85% market share. Univac, which had concentrated on its engineering and technical skills, held a mere 10% of the market — the rest being shared by Burroughs, NCR and RCA. IBM has maintained its market leadership for over a quarter of a century.[1]

Although BIC took the initiative by creating the volume market for disposable razors and lighters in the US, Gillette was able to mount a successful counter-attack. Gillette concentrated its resources on outpromoting BIC and, due to Gillette's existing well developed distribution organization, little emphasis was required to distribute the disposables. In contrast, BIC was new to the market and needed to split its resources between promotion and establishing a national distribution network. BIC did not have the resources to win a two-front battle and leadership went to Gillette through its use of a skilful defensive strategy.

Minnetonka, a small regional soap manufacturer, was too small to take on the market leaders in a frontal attack and used a flanking strategy — segmentation with a new product concept — to outmanœuvre its rivals. In 1979, Minnetonka introduced Softsoap, a liquid soap in a plastic bottle with a pump dispenser. Softsoap was an immediate consumer success and created a new market worth almost $65 million a year by 1981. The introduction of Softsoap caught the major bar soap manufacturers, Colgate–Palmolive, Lever and Procter & Gamble, completely by surprise and without a counter–weapon to combat the audacious interloper.[2]

During and after the 1973 oil embargo the major oil companies, with the exception of Texaco, changed their strategy from refining to exploration and from increasing the sale of refined products to diversification. Through to 1978, Texaco was still fighting the old battle to win refinery and distribution sales rather than the new battle to find new oil supplies and spread business risk. As a consequence of fighting the wrong battle, Texaco's profits fell from first to seventh among the major oil companies.[3]

The common denominator in these examples is that the success of a company in markets ranging from high technology to consumer and commodity products, was dependent on principles common to military strategy. The close relationship of strategic principles is based on the fact that the theory of market conflict closely resembles the power politics theory of conflict. Market conflict arises from the corporate pursuit of incompatible goals involving the security, power and prestige of other companies in the market. The company is a unique sovereign unit and there is a lack of truly enforceable constraints on company–to–company behaviour in the market–place. Market conflict is the result of miscalculations by executives — as with Xerox' entry into and later withdrawal from, the mainframe computer market — or the over concentration of power in the market–place. The profit and growth opportunities offered by the explosive growth of the personal computer market attracted heavy competition against the originator and leader, Apple. Conflict can be avoided in the market–place by maintaining the balance of power, deterrence, agreement on spheres of influence (which are generally illegal), and judicious attention to corporate security and interests. The instruments of application of strategies, companies and armies, are parallelisms. Companies and armies are remarkably similar in objectives and organizational concepts and companies subconsciously emulate the systems, principles, manœuvres, functions, structures, procedures, and even the language, training and behaviour of armies.

OBJECTIVES

Companies and armies do not want conflict — but they do want the market share (territory) and the profits (spoils) that go with it. The objective of a war in the market–place or on the battlefield is to attain a better state of peace for the instigator. Wars break out in the market–place when one company calculates that it has more to gain than lose by aggression, intimidation or subversion. Company security is market leadership and market share; company sovereignty is its customers, resources and ownership from which it derives its relative power. Any challenge to the security, sovereignty and power of a company is a declaration of war.

SYSTEMS

Companies and armies are competitive systems which jockey for advantage over adversaries. In essence, they both seek to upset the status quo, shifting relationships and re–establishing an equilibrium more favourable to the aggressor. As Leon Sampson observed; 'War is a transfer of property from nation to nation'. In business warfare, that property is market share, customers, resources, or ownership.

PRINCIPLES

Companies obey the same basic principles of combat used by their military counterparts. Both are goal–orientated and both recognize that taking the initiative can provide a crucial advantage; that the concentration of resources are decisive for a breakthrough; that economy is as essential as the manœuvrability and co–ordination of resources; that security prevents surprise; that surprise moves vastly increase the chances of success and that simplicity of objectives, form, systems and instructions, avoiding the pressures of complexity, hones a fine cutting edge — a bias for action.

MANŒUVRES

The deterrent, attack, defence and alliance manœuvres, undertaken by companies in response to actual or perceived aggression in the market–place, are analogous to those taken by the military on the battlefield.

FUNCTIONS

Firms, like armies, require weapons — manufacturing, marketing, financial and technological as well as human resources — and skills to fight. They need intelligence on both the adversary and the market environment. They use internal communications for information transfer and employ external communications for propaganda. Logistics are needed to move produce and services to the market-place, and leadership and organization to direct and motivate employees, and to implement tactics.

STRUCTURES

Companies and armies are tribal societies employing hierarchical organization structures and behaviour patterns including value systems — culture and attitudes which have been institutionalized by example and passed on to succeeding generations, and hardened by success into custom.

PROCEDURES

Manuals and operating procedures have been adopted by companies and armies to rationalize and standardize activities under conflict. The drafting of, for example, financial statements or maps are rigorously standardized so that others will be able to read and interpret them in exactly the same way throughout the organization under any conditions.

BEHAVIOUR

Employees and troops are preconditioned through training and procedures to order, obedience and uniform behaviour. By organizing the intake of sensations, reducing the events of conflict to a few easily recognizable sets of elements, and providing the employees and troops with sets of appropriate responses, the firm or army can overcome the disorientation of noise and smoke in the market-place and on the battlefield, avoid fatal shocks and surprises and still continue to function as a cohesive entity.

LANGUAGE

The language of companies and armies describes the nature of conflict, and military terminology has been widely adopted by companies. Terms such as advertising 'campaigns', 'battles' for market share, a promotional 'blitz', and the sales 'force' are a few of the evocative terms employed by companies every day in business to characterize market conflict.

TRAINING

Companies and armies both use in-house basic training, specialist skills courses, and management development programmes as an integral feature of organizational development. Basic training in Matsushita has its parallels in army recruit training. Specialist skills developed in the General Motors Institute's apprenticeship programmes have their equivalent in army trade schools. Middle management programmes at McDonalds' Hamburger University emulate those at infantry schools, and senior management programmes at BAT or IBM can be compared to those at Sandhurst, Saint-Cyr or West Point.

Given the organizational and competitive similarities between companies and armies, and the nature of conflict in the market-place, the study of military strategy, with its proven record of success under combat conditions, is of great value to the executive.

Probably at no time in the recent past has business been so competitive with the emphasis on survival and growth under adversity. In fact, business is on a war footing. In declining markets, business success rests on timing the disengagement and withdrawing in good order, or of finding a new way to win. In mature or low growth markets, success depends on taking market territory or share away from rivals. In growth markets, companies are confronted with carving-out and holding a territorial claim in the market in the face of opposition from a myriad of competitors, all eager for the spoils.

Companies fail in the market-place for precisely the same reasons that armies fail on the battlefield. As Lord Wavell remarked, 'wars are won by those who make the fewest mistakes'. Companies which select inappropriate strategies, lack resources, are badly led, have poor weapons or inadequate supplies and training, lack knowledge, or are poorly motivated will fail just as readily in the market as will a similarly configured army on the battlefield. Those success factors critical to the business executive are the same as those crucial to military commanders.

Military experience is a veritable goldmine of competitive strategies, all well tested under combat conditions; so much so, indeed, that the captain of industry can learn much from the captain of war.

This book is about applying tested military strategies to business to win battles in the market-place.

Source References

1.   The Economist, June 19, 1982.
2.   The New York Times, November 1, 1981.
3.   The Financial Times, October 8, 1981.

chapter two
STRATEGY: THE CONDUCT OF CONFLICT

'Strategy is the art of distributing and applying military means to fulfil the ends of policy'.

Sir Basil Liddell Hart

Strategy is the managerial cult-word of the 1980s. Yet few managers really understand what strategy is, the levels of strategic decision making, nor the various approaches to strategy.

This chapter introduces the major strategic concepts used in this book and illustrates the similarities between military and business strategy, to provide an insight into the use of the basic strategic military manœuvres in business which are explored in succeeding chapters.

STRATEGY — A DEFINITION

Strategy is the set of policies used for the conduct of conflict. Since both armies and companies are competitive systems trying to secure an advantage over adversaries, they are conflict orientated and strategy is used as the policy tool for planning aggression against opponents. The sole objective of armies and companies in conflict is to outmanœuvre their opponents and gain a superior position on the battlefield or in the market-place.

Simply defined, strategy is the organized deployment of resources to achieve specific objectives against competition from rival organizations.

THE HIERARCHY OF STRATEGY

Armies and companies operate at three discrete levels of strategy (see Figure 2.1).

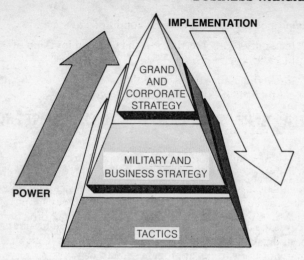

Figure 2.1
THE HIERARCHY OF STRATEGY

Grand Strategy and Corporate Strategy

The highest levels of strategy are grand (political) and corporate (business) strategy, both of which are concerned with the use of resources to pursue specific organizational objectives.

Grand strategy is a set of policies developed by governments to guide the conduct of war. Grand strategy co-ordinates and directs all resources towards the achievement of the political objective of war. Grand strategy develops the economic resources necessary to sustain the combat elements, fosters morale to maintain commitment, regulates the distribution of power between the various elements, and applies the country's resources in such a way as to weaken the opponent's will to fight. Since grand strategy is a policy tool, the decision of the USSR to declare war on Japan in the final days of the Second World War was typical of an interventionist policy designed to secure an advantage. The minimal object of grand strategy is to preserve the state within its own frontiers and its political, economic and social systems. War occurs between states when these minimal objectives come into dispute, or when one state has aspirations on another state's territory or systems. Typical examples of conflict under these conditions are:

> the annexation of territory — the German invasion of Poland in 1939;

> threats to change the socio–political system — the Vietnamese conflicts, 1945—1954 and 1964—1975;

> attempting to obtain economic advantage — the European colonial wars of the 17th and 18th centuries.

The direct business parallel with grand strategy is corporate strategy. Corporate strategy is the use of all the firm's resources — financial, technological, production, marketing and manpower — to pursue a corporate objective. It is a set of policies adopted by the board of directors which guides the scope and direction of a company. Corporate strategy is the central management tool for coping with both the internal and external changes that a firm faces, and is concerned with the scope and development of resources among the portfolio of businesses in which the company participates to meet the overall business objectives of the firm. For example, a corporate policy for RCA was to both enter, and later, abandon the mainframe computer industry as the perceived business opportunity turned into an actual threat. As a corporate strategy, Philip Morris used the profit from Marlboro cirgarettes, with sales of $3.5 billion a year (35% of the total annual revenues of $11 billion) to finance the acquisition and revamping of Miller Brewing Company in 1970 and Seven-Up in 1978.[1]

Corporate strategy develops the economic resources necessary to sustain the portfolio of business, fosters morale, regulates the distribution of financial power between the various businesses, and applies the firm's resources to weaken the opponent's will to fight. The minimal objective of corporate strategy is to preserve the company's position within the boundaries of its business activities, and its ownership and organization structure. Conflict occurs between companies when these minimal objectives are disputed, or when one firm has aspirations which conflict with this equilibrium. Typical examples of conflict under these conditions are:

> the entry into a company's market of a new competitor who upsets market equilibrium — Airbus Industries' A300B wide-bodied jet airliner entering the market which was formerly the

preserve of Boeing, Lockheed, and McDonnell–Douglas;

threats to change the ownership — Continental Airline's unsuccessful bid in 1981 to fight off Texas International Airline's acquisition of the controlling interest in the former;

obtaining economic advantage — the scramble of companies to obtain leases for gas and oil prospecting in the North Sea, many from consortia who were formerly not involved in either the oil or gas industries.

Military Strategy and Business Strategy

Military strategy deals with campaigns where military means are used to attain the national objective, and is predicated on physical action or threatened physical action, using force of arms to secure a victory.

The distinction between military and grand strategy is that the latter controls the former, since military strategy is one component of grand strategy which, if successfully conducted, can alleviate the need for force of arms. Military strategy is the province of generals while grand strategy is the province of statesmen.

Business strategy is concerned with achieving specific objectives within a particular business, such as electronic calculators; or in a market, such as Germany; or in a specific product segment, like packaged table–salt; or a combination of geographic and product markets within a business area. Business strategy objectives are directed towards achieving corporate objectives such as producing a specific contribution of sales revenue, income and earnings per share. As in the military sense, the objectives of a corporate strategy, determined by the board of directors, control a business unit's strategy and are implemented by operating management. Business strategy is a plan for resource deployment to support a corporate objective, together with a system of measures for its accomplishment.

Ford, General Motors and Volkswagen are using resource deployment strategies as part of a programme to counter Japanese attacks on their car business in Europe and North America. All three companies have extensive production facilities in Brazil, and are using their low production cost advantage in Brazil to manufacture and ship components to Europe and North America, to help offset the overall steel and labour cost advantage enjoyed by

Japanese car manufacturers. Although there is an adage which suggests that battles are won or lost at the tactical level, since there are no victories in strategy, this is not strictly true. While the Battle of Jutland (1916) was considered a tactical failure by the British since they lost more ships than the Germans, the engagement was a strategic success since the German high seas fleet remained in port for the rest of the First World War. Similarly, in business, while selling tyres to car manufacturers at marginal cost may appear to be a tactical failure, it is strategically successful. The original equipment market generates high volume business for the tyre manufacturers which facilitates low unit costs, and being part of the original equipment encourages consumers to select the same types for replacement thereby providing high unit margins for the manufacturers in the replacement tyre market.

Tactics

Tactics concern the conduct of forces in battle. Tactics, in a military sense, is the employment of troops in battle and differs from military strategy primarily in scope. The best definition of this distinction was given by Von Clausewitz; 'Tactics is the art of using troops in battle; strategy is the art of using battles to win wars'. In business, tactics are a set of action programmes designed to fulfil business strategy, and are concerned with the *employment* of resources such as sales forces, advertising, and production capacity, rather than the *deployment* of resources.

Business tactics are the tools used to achieve a business strategy, and success in business, as in war, depends largely on the quality of the implementation of tactics. If the sales force cannot sell a product effectively the objective to become market leader will not be reached.

STRATEGIC APPROACHES

Military and business planners adopt a number of similar strategic approaches to conflict.

Sequential Strategies

Sequential strategies are successive steps, each contingent on the preceding step, that lead to the final objective.

Efforts to undermine an enemy's morale, isolate him from allies, deny him external supplies, and destroy his internal lines of communication before invading his homeland, is a typical sequential strategy. Control of the sea lanes, local air superiority, harassing commando raids, and intense sea and air bombardment denying resupply and casualty evacuation which contributed to low morale, was a sequential strategy adopted by the British, designed to set the stage for a series of successful landings to reoccupy the Falkland Islands in May 1982.

The Japanese pharmaceutical companies are using a sequential strategy to become a major force in the world drug market (see Figure 2.2). Initially, the research and development (R&D) effort was expanded to provide access to indigenous drugs; these new drugs were then licensed out to non-Japanese pharmaceutical companies to produce royalty income to further increase R&D. Joint ventures followed with non-Japanese firms in several major countries to gain market experience, which in turn was followed by selective acquisition of local companies to secure control of local marketing and distribution as a means to maximize future downstream revenue.[2]

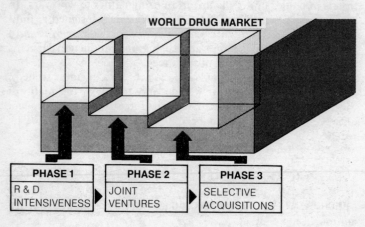

Figure 2.2
SEQUENTIAL STRATEGY
The Japanese pharmaceutical companies' sequential strategy to penetrate the world drug market.

Cumulative Strategies

Cumulative strategies are a collection of seemingly random, but planned, actions which eventually create crushing results.

The Russian occupation of nine European countries between 1945 and 1948, while not a threat on an individual basis, in combination posed a serious strategic threat to Western European security.

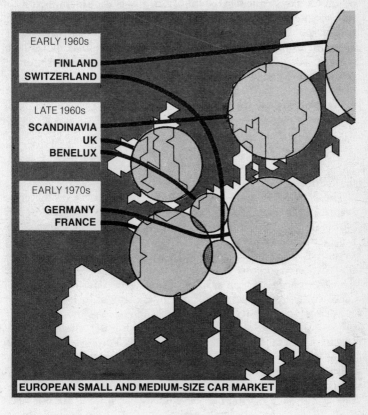

EARLY 1960s

FINLAND
SWITZERLAND

LATE 1960s

SCANDINAVIA
UK
BENELUX

EARLY 1970s

GERMANY
FRANCE

EUROPEAN SMALL AND MEDIUM-SIZE CAR MARKET

Figure 2.3
CUMULATIVE STRATEGY
The Japanese car companies' cumulative attack on the European car market to increase share over time and open up new markets.

The Japanese automobile manufacturers followed a cumulative strategy to penetrate the European market for small and medium-sized passenger cars (see Figure 2.3). Early market entries in countries with no indigenous passenger car production (Finland and Switzerland) in the early 1960s was followed by penetration into markets in the Benelux, Scandinavia and the UK in the late 1960s, and by France and Germany in the early 1970s. By 1973 the Japanese had secured 3.7% of the European car market. While no one market was critical to the European automobile manufacturers, by the late 1970s they were presented with a viable Japanese competitive position (based purely on imported cars) throughout Western Europe. The Japanese successfully built upon their cumulative strategy and almost tripled their European market share in the next decade to 9.6%.[3]

Indirect Strategies

Indirect or deterrent strategies use psychological pressures to defeat an enemy and thereby avoid 'physical' conflict. They emphasize political, economic, social and psychological pressures instead of force, and attempt to throw an enemy off balance before engaging the main force.

The North Vietnamese made considerable use of the psychological pressures of world opinion to halt the US bombing of the North in 1968. By halting the bombing, the North Vietnamese removed a military threat which they could not oppose effectively by military means, relieving pressures on internal lines of communication, troop movements, and supply bases. When linked to the US disengagement in 1972, this provided the decisive element in successfully overthrowing the Thieu government in 1975.

Boeing successfully employed psychological and economic pressures to avoid a 'physical' contest with other aircraft manufacturers with the 747 aircraft (see Figure 2.4). The development cost of the 747, some two billion dollars in the 1960s, was then the largest private funding of a civilian jet airliner. There was a limited demand for routes for a 350—400 seat intercontinental airliner in the late 1960s, and once Boeing had developed such a large aircraft with high development cost and limited market, it would have been economic suicide for another aircraft manufacturer to produce a directly competing plane. Both IBM and Xerox successfully used indirect strategies to achieve early domination of the mainframe computer and photocopier markets, respectively. Both companies created a major financial barrier to potential competitors by leasing rather than selling computers and photocopiers. To enter the market and compete successfully, challengers required access to large amounts of working capital to finance both the leasing arrangements and fund extensive R&D.

(Chapter Three deals in more detail with indirect strategies as deterrents.)

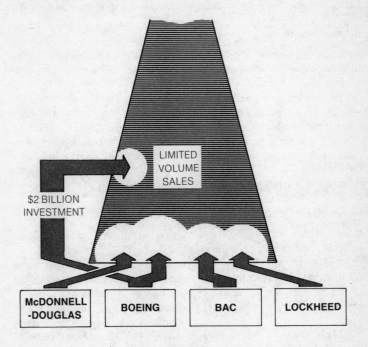

Figure 2.4
INDIRECT STRATEGY

Boeing Airplane Company's indirect strategy based on psychological and economic deterrents for the long-range, capacity 747.

Direct Strategies

Direct strategies employ direct physical force to achieve objectives and are the most common form of military strategy, being present in almost all wars throughout history.

Direct strategies in business, involving an attack with a new market entrant, or the defence of a market from competitive attack, typify the business strategy adopted for almost all products and services in the market–place (see Figure 2.5). Chapters Four and Five are concerned with direct offensive and defensive strategies.

Alliance Strategies

Alliance strategies are attempts to outmanœuvre opponents through a combination of the resources of several combatants with similar objectives.

Fujitsu's alliances with ICL and Siemens in Europe and Amdahl in the USA, for example, provide for the supply of Fujitsu's computer products and technology, and for joint marketing through powerful local companies who are in a better position to counter the strong capabilities of multinational competitors like IBM.
(Chapter Six explores alliance strategies in depth.)

Counterforce Strategies

Counterforce strategies are designed to destroy or neutralize selected military capabilities of an enemy. Typical military examples are the use of precision bombing to destroy communications centres and armaments plants. An excellent example of the modern use of counterforce strategy is the Israeli's use of electronic counter–measure (ECM) equipment to neutralize, and 'smart' bombs to destroy, the Egyptians' surface–to–air missile (SAM) batteries in the Yom Kippur War (1973) which had initially limited the Israeli's use of tactical air power to stem the Egyptian invasion of Sinai.

In business, typical counterforce strategies used to selectively neutralize an opponent would be challenges to patents, trademarks, copyright, and advertising claims of an opponent, and the introduction of rival products.

AGie, the Swiss wire cutting machine tool firm, has successfully used counterforce strategies to combat Japanese patent violations of

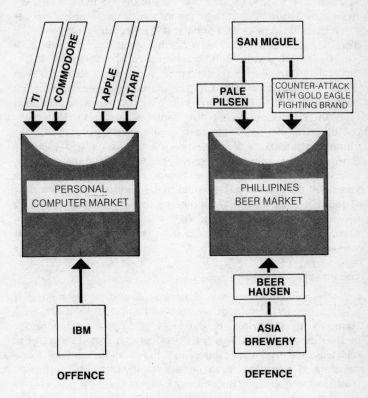

Figure 2.5
DIRECT STRATEGIES
Attack and defence

its unique wire-cut spark erosion technology in the US, which enabled its competitors, using similar technology at prices 20% to 30% below AGie's, to capture over 50% of the US market. In 1981, AGie took action against these patent violations; winning an out-of-court settlement from Fanuc in 1981, securing compensation from Hitachi Seiko in 1982 (together totalling $5 million in compensation), and bringing a suit against Mitsubishi in 1982.[4]

A classic counterforce manœuvre was employed by IBM in retaliation to Xerox' entry into the mainframe computer market dominated by IBM (see Figure 2.6). While Xerox' XDS computer division was locked in all-out frontal assault on IBM in the computer market, IBM launched a competitive product into the photocopier market, dominated by Xerox, which had used the profits from its copier and copy paper sales to fund the attack on IBM in the mainframe computer market. IBM's product was its own version of the most popular model in the middle of the Xerox line which IBM rented at a price well below that of Xerox. Faced with a two-front war of attrition and IBM's threat to neutralize Xerox' prime source of income, the XDS, after several years of losses, was sold out to Honeywell by Xerox.

Countervalue Strategies

Countervalue strategies are designed to destroy or neutralize selected enemy population centres, industrial capabilities, or a country's infrastructure. The RAF and USAAF were used in Europe in the Second World War as a strategic weapon to neutralize selected industrial capabilities and the communications infrastructure of Germany, as a prelude to invading the European mainland and ultimately defeating Germany.

The business actions closest to military countervalue strategies are firms neutralizing a rival's customer base, by providing unique services, or neutralizing raw material sources by obtaining or controlling access to raw materials. Boots, for example, when attacking Upjohn's identical anti-arthritic drug (Motrin) with their Rufen brand in the US, used an unconventional approach in the prescription drug market by using penetration pricing advertised directly to consumers to neutralize Motrin's customer base (see Figure 2.7). Since Motrin's patients were largely elderly, on fixed incomes and used the product long-term, there were major financial incentives for customers to switch to a lower cost

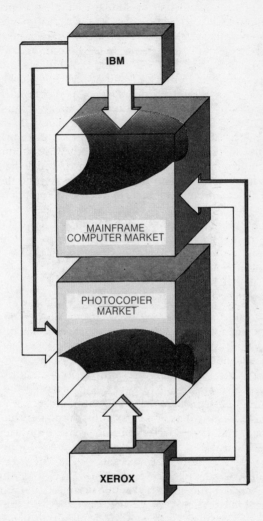

Figure 2.6
COUNTERFORCE STRATEGY

IBM's attack on Xerox' photocopier business in response to Xerox' offence against IBM in the mainframe computer market.

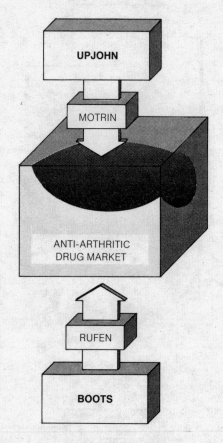

Figure 2.7
COUNTERVALUE STRATEGY
Boot's attack with Rufen on Upjohn, using penetration pricing to neutralize Motrin's customer base.

alternative. Boots' astute pricing policy and targeted promotion switched many customers from Motrin to Rufen. The local bottler of Pepsi-Cola in Iran, during the late 1960s, successfully neutralized Coca-Cola's sales offensive. The bottler purchased the sole Iranian glass bottle plant, succeeded in having high tariffs erected against imported glass bottles, and introduced a return fee on Coca-Cola bottles delivered to the Pepsi bottling plant. This countervalue strategy effectively neutralized Coca-Cola's supply of essential packaging materials, and allowed Pepsi to become undisputed market leader.

Counterforce and countervalue strategies are frequently part of offensive and defensive manoeuvres and are illustrated in Chapters Four and Five.

In the competition for power and position on the battlefield and in the market-place, armies and companies use four basic strategic responses in conflict situations. Deterrent strategies are used to prevent an attack; offensive strategies to attack competitors; defensive strategies to protect against the attacks of adversaries; and alliances to form deterrent, defensive and offensive positions against their opponents. Chapters Three to Six explore these basic manoeuvres and their sub-strategies in both a military and business context to illustrate the wide range of strategic moves and counter moves open to the executive facing market conflict.

It is essential to recognize that in both military and business conflict, armies and companies invariably adopt a combination of sub-strategies which straddle a number of discrete strategic manoeuvres. For example, in a typical attack on a market leader, discrete sub-strategies are used for price, credit, product quality, volume, distribution, advertising, promotion, sales force deployment, and after-sales servicing, all of which relate back to the central strategic offensive theme. The cases depicted in the text, while essentially illustrating one strategic manoeuvre, generally form part of an overall strategic response of which the illustrated manoeuvre is one, but a key, component.

Source References

1.   The Wall Street Journal, June 30, 1982.
2.   The Economist, June 5, 1981.
3.   Business Week, August 6, 1984.
4.   Business Week, August 29, 1983.

chapter three
DETERRENCE

> 'The supreme act of war is to subdue the enemy *without* fighting'.
>
> Sun Tzu

The concept of deterrence is as old as military conflict. Deterrence is a strategy to prevent conflict, by persuading a rational competitor that you are willing and able to punish non-compliance with your clearly expressed and understood wishes. Deterrence is a strategy for an acceptable peace rather than a war, and is a battle won in the mind of the competitor through psychological pressure rather than by physical combat. It depends largely on intuition and emotion as opposed to logic, and requires an army or firm to induce a competitor to co-operate by voluntary restraint.

Conflict occurs when a competitor anticipates that the risk is low in relation to the gain from a planned aggressive move, or from an impulsive act. An effective deterrent strategy must discourage combat in either form and must deal with direct attacks, extremely provocative acts, and aggressive adventurism.

DIRECT ATTACKS

Hitler successfully gambled that Britain and France would not react to the German invasion of the Sudetenland, and later the occupation of all Czechoslovakia (1939). Cheseborough–Ponds correctly anticipated that by launching a new product into a market of small importance to a major manufacturer, spectacular results could be achieved. Cheseborough launched Rave into the then $40 million US market for home permanents dominated by Gillette's Toni. Rave, a superior product containing no ammonia and with no smell, backed by a small but skilful marketing programme, increased the market to $100 million by 1981 and Rave took brand leadership away from Toni.[1]

EXTREMELY PROVOCATIVE ACTS

Hitler's re-occupation of the Rheinland in 1936 was an extremely
provocative act, which was not deterred by the presence of the
superior forces of the French. Duracell's entrance into the battery
market in the United Kingdom, which was dominated by Ever-
Ready with an 85% share, was an extremely provocative act.
Duracell gambled correctly that Ever-Ready would emphasize its
traditional strength in the declining zinc-carbon battery segment
rather than in the growing alkaline segment, and would maintain its
traditional distribution through specialist retailers rather than open
up mass merchandising through supermarkets. Within two years,
Ever Ready's market share had fallen to 65% and the newcomer,
Duracell, by using new technology and new distribution techniques, had reached 22%.[2]

AGGRESSIVE ADVENTURISM

The use of pseudo-volunteers by the Cubans supported by massive
supplies of material to Angola during the civil war in 1976, was an
act of aggressive adventurism which was not successfully deterred.
The Japanese car manufacturers correctly anticipated that their
cumulative strategy for the envelopment of the European car
market, started in the early 1960s, would not be deterred by either
competitors or European governments until the aggressive adventure was essentially complete.

ELEMENTS OF DETERRENCE

Four key elements are present in all effective deterrent stategies
whether for war or business.

1. *Credibility.*
Where a company convinces a competitor that it is willing to inflict
unacceptable losses on the competitor to further its aims or to
maintain its position, and that the competitor has something to gain
from restraint. If the competitor is willing to accept the risk of
punishment, the threat is obviously not regarded as credible.

   Following the 1967 Arab-Israeli war, the Israelis have been
successful in persuading the Jordanians to avoid military confrontation as the risks outweigh the benefits.

   In the mid-1970s, VFW-Fokker signalled British Aerospace
(BAe) that it would not tolerate their projected HS-146 aircraft in

direct competition with Fokker's existing F-28 short-haul jet airliner. Fokker indicated that over 40% of the total cost of both their F-27 and F-28 aircraft was supplied by British companies and at risk if the HS-146 project went ahead. BAe correctly gauged that the threat was not credible since re-design, re-tooling, and re-certification costs for both aircraft using non-British equipment would be prohibitive to Fokker. The HS-146 project went ahead. In contrast, Texas Instruments successfully used credibility to win a battle for future supply. In 1981, TI announced a price for random access memory (RAM) chips to be marketed in 1983. Bowmar offered a lower price for RAM chips with the same characteristics within a week, which was followed by Motorola with an even lower price three weeks later. Two weeks after Motorola's offer, TI announced a new price one-half of that offered by Motorola. TI won the battle even before the product was manufactured through its proven credibility as the lowest cost producer.

2. *Capability*.

Where a company convinces a competitor that, in addition to being willing, it has the means and the resources to carry out the threat of punishment.

While the US has successfully deterred the North Koreans from re-invading South Korea since 1953, by maintaining combat elements in South Korea, the vastly superior US military capability did not deter the Iranians during the embassy hostage crisis (1979—1981) since the US was not dealing with a rational opponent.

While IMS has been able to deter competitors from entering the pharmacy and hospital audit markets for drug products on virtually a world-wide basis, due to high start-up costs and a limited customer base, A.C. Nielsen, with the dominant position in the $100 million US televison audience measurement markets, has been unable to deter competition. Despite Nielsen's imposing technological prowess, innovative use of sophisticated data handling and analysis, and formidable legacy of historical data, AGB of the UK and Times' Sales Area Marketing, McGraw-Hill's Data Resources and Control Data's Arbitron subsidiaries were not deterred by Nielsen's capabilities, and all successfully penetrated Nielsen's US markets.[3]

3. *Communication*.

Where a company clearly signals a competitor of the intention to further its aims or maintain its position, and makes the competitor fully aware of any benefits available in co-operaton as well as punishments that may be meted out for non-compliance.

While the United States succeeded in removing the Russian missile threat in Cuba in 1962 through successful communication of its intentions, the United States was not able to communicate effectively enough to initially deter or subsequently engineer the withdrawal of the Russian forces which invaded Afghanistan in late 1979.

IBM, in the mid-1960s, made a widespread product announcement of its 360 series computer, promising a level of performance far exceeding current competitors two to three years before the 360 series was commercially available. This had the effect of deterring customers from making an immediate purchase decision for existing competitive computers (CDC's 6600 and Honeywell's H-200) by enticing them to wait for the new advanced IBM 360 series. In contrast, the US truck manufacturers, in the 1979—81, period were unsuccessful in signalling the poor operating economics and low margins of the medium-sized truck market in the USA, to deter market entrance by Daimler-Benz, IMAC, Renault and Volvo. Due to the economic situation in Europe, these companies were facing problems in their home markets, and looked to the US market as a way of reviving depressed demand. By ineffective communication, the US manufacturers were forced to fight additional new competitors in a weak truck market.[4]

4. *Rationality.*
Where a company, although acting arbitrarily and unreasonably, avoids arousing emotion on the part of a competitor. By persuading the competitor to act in a rational, reasonable, and objective manner to avoid foregoing any benefits of co-operation, the competitor is at a disadvantage. Rationality is the key to an effective deterrence strategy. However, actual or potential competitors do not always act in a rational manner. While the Israelis have been able to persuade the Jordanians to act rationally since the Six Day War in 1967, they have failed to get the Syrians to act in a similar fashion.

IBM's introduction of its advanced *Displaywriter* line of word processors in mid-1980 did not force all its twenty-odd competitors to act rationally when faced with a superior product and the power of IBM's sales and service organization. Some firms counter-attacked by introducing new, better, and less expensive models as a direct response, while other firms, faced with shrinking profit margins and volumes, acted rationally and looked for mergers or left the market.[5]

DETERRENT STRATEGIES

Deterrent strategies in business consist of a number of marketing, production, financial, technological, and managerial sub-strategies, designed to prevent competitors from upsetting market equilibrium by creating real or perceived entry barriers and profit-taking hurdles (see Table 3.1).

Marketing Deterrents

Distribution
Japanese companies have successfully used the complexity of the distribution system in Japan to deter potential competitors from distributing themselves in favour of using the local system or a local Japanese partner. This strategy has produced another layer of costs for the foreign competitor to absorb and, together with removing the new company from the customer, has made foreign firms less competitive than their Japanese counterparts.

Promotion
A hallmark of Proctor & Gamble in the US is its massive advertising and promotion budget — over $500 million on media alone in 1981 — which is used to buy and maintain its market share. This acts as a strong deterrent to many companies seeking to enter or increase their share in markets dominated by P&G products.[6]

Franchise
Hewlett–Packard (H–P) has built a strong reputation over the years, with major manufacturing companies like Boeing and General Motors, by supplying high quality electronic test and measurement instruments. H–P's reputation among such companies was sufficient to deter them from purchasing rival minicomputers in favour of the H–P models, from a firm that they knew and trusted.[7]

Service
Pitney–Bowes' 92% share of the postage meter market in the US is due in part to the 7,500–person sales and service force which calls on thousands of small firms. Despite encouragement from the US

MARKETING DETERRENTS

- Distribution
- Promotion
- Franchise
- Service
- Quality
- Pricing

PRODUCTION DETERRENTS

- Capacity
- Utilization
- Equipment

FINANCIAL DETERRENTS

- Costs
- Economics

TECHNOLOGICAL DETERRENTS

- Innovation
- Information

MANAGERIAL DETERRENTS

- Acquisitions
- Mergers
- Alliances

Table 3.1
KEY DETERRENT STRATEGIES

Justice Department, few firms want to enter a market so dominated by one company's product and its sales and service force.[8]

Quality
Swissair has successfully deterred US-based carriers from competing profitably on the scheduled Swiss—US air routes following TWA's withdrawal in the mid-1970s. Swissair skilfully maintained prices, matched demand closely with capacity, and offered a world-beating in-flight cabin service, all of which deterred potential competitors.

Pricing
Bausch & Lomb, in the soft contact lens market in the US, deterred competitors by drastically reducing prices and pushing for wider distribution, which changed the product from a speciality to a price-sensitive mass-market item. The majority of competitors were small firms who were financially unable to match the changed economics of the market and the new distribution system, and sought buyers for their companies.[9]

Production Deterrents

Capacity
Hoffmann-La Roche successfully deterred existing and potential competitors in the bulk vitamin C market by building production capacity to meet world demand. This intimidated many competitors by creating the spectre of the lowest cost supplier able to meet and win any price war, to the extent that many withdrew from the market. By 1980, Roche accounted for some 60% of the world market for vitamin C.

Utilization
In the free-for-all following airline de-regulation in the US, a few regional carriers, such as Piedmont, Southwest, and US Air, increased capacity with more frequent services at lower prices on existing routes to deter competition. Since the airline with the most flights on a route gets a disproportionate share of traffic, and the load factor determines profitability, many new low-fare airlines were deterred from competing on these routes.[10]

Equipment
Kodak's monopoly on film for its Disc camera forced film processing companies to either purchase special, relatively expen-

sive, processing equipment from Kodak or to hand over their Disc film processing business to Kodak's own facilities. Either way, Kodak has maintained a strong profit position in the Disc film processing business by deterring direct competition.[11]

Financial Deterrents

Costs

Existing semiconductor firms have successfully deterred new competitors from entering the industry due to the high cost of participation. In the early 1970s, new manufacturing facilities cost up to $5 million. By 1982, the cost of a single new plant to build advanced VLSI 64K RAM chips was between $60 and $120 million, creating a high entrance fee for new competitors.[12]

Economics

Federal Express is the leading and lowest cost air courier service in the US. Federal Express' overnight letter service was introduced in 1981 at a low price with the aim of becoming profitable on volume in a 12-month period. Competitors were deterred from entering the overnight letter market due to the difficulty in making money against the lowest cost competitor using marginal costing and penetration pricing.[13]

Technological Deterrents

Innovation

The high-risk, long-run, and high-cost business cycle of the pharmaceutical industry, where the number of products reaching the market is small, the discovery-to-marketing time is an average of twelve years, and development costs are in the range of $50 million to $100 million per product, has deterred all but the largest new companies from entering the market. In fact, no totally new company to the drug market has succeeded, from start up, in becoming a medium-size pharmaceutical firm in the last thirty years, with the exceptions of Janssen and Syntex.

Information

IBM is believed to delay the release of new product specifications, to provide itself with a lead time over competitors seeking to supply compatible equipment to plug into new IBM computers, deterring an immediate response from plug-compatible competitors.[14]

Managerial Deterrents

Acquisitions

Firms use both vertical and horizontal integration as a deterrent. By integrating upstream, a firm can secure control over production and supply sources. Tube Investments in the UK integrated backwards by buying into steel making when the industry was first de-nationalized in 1953. Tube Investments obtained security of raw materials and the profits made by its suppliers, and deterred its competitors. By integrating downstream, a firm can secure control of distribution or other benefits. Genentech, a leading bio-technology company, is integrating forward from research into production as a means to limit the transfer of critical purification know-how, to deter current clients from becoming future competitors. By horizontal integration, firms attempt to envelop the market to deter competitors. In the US, fast food market firms try to obtain the first franchise in new shopping malls, to deter other fast food companies from opening up competitive outlets. All integration strategies have the potential to deny competitive access to raw materials, know-how, and customers, and can be powerful deterrents.

Mergers

Thomson–Brandt of France acquired 75% of AEG–Telefunken's television and video–recorder subsidiary in 1983. The merged entity held 25% of the German and 20% of the European colour TV markets, and 10% of the German video–recorder market. Brandt's strategy was designed to build a large European consumer electronics group with 1982 sales of $2.6 billion, capable of competing with, and deterring, further Japanese penetration of the European consumer electronics market.

Alliances

None of the three leading jet aero–engine manufacturers — General Electric (GE), Pratt & Whitney (P&W), and Rolls–Royce — were willing to fund alone the development of a new fuel–efficient engine, to power a 150–seat airliner at an estimated development cost of $1.5 billion. But equally, each could not face the prospects of competing against the two other manufacturers for the same market. Each of the firms attempted to form alliances with smaller firms (GE with Snecma, P&W with MTU and Fiat Aviazione and

Rolls–Royce with Kawasaki, Mitsubishi and IHI) in an effort to deter the others from entering the market. In early 1983, Pratt & Whitney formed a consortium with Rolls–Royce where the former, with MTU and Fiat, would design and build the gearbox and turbines, and Rolls–Royce and its Japanese partners would build the fan and compressors for the new V–2500 engine.[15]

SUMMARY

Deterrent strategies in business attempt to induce stability by encouraging prudence on the part of competitors. This stability, rather than signifying the ability of combatants to inflict equal damage on each other, reflects their ability to inflict unacceptable losses on one another in the worst case and, under less violent circumstances, a greater loss for the challenger. To effectively deter a competitive thrust, a firm must present a credible and visible case to convince competitors that challenges to the market equilibrium will be met, and that beyond a certain point the challenge is not in the long–term interests of the aggressor. In many respects deterrent strategies are based on a network of visible minefields of company strengths or advantages which are designed, and displayed, to discourage competitive aggression (see Figure 3.1). If a company is not prepared to fight a war in the market–place it cannot rationally or credibly threaten a competitor, and its own survival is threatened if it adopts a deterrent strategy. The most critical factor in a deterrent strategy is gauging the capabilities and intentions of a challenger which, since full information can never be obtained, must be imprecise. Capabilities in terms of management, products, and resources constantly change and are not entirely tangible, but can be determined with some degree of objectivity. Intentions are a state of mind and can only be gauged subjectively. Measurement of intention depends on judging the interests and objectives of competitors and the temperament and will of a challenger's management. Companies frequently appear to be unaware that market conflict has psychological and emotional dimensions, as well as a physical component, and that being able to predict, and effectively counter, competitive moves is a major strategic task.

Unlike the military, little research has been conducted to identify the intentions of a competitor's management and their psychological and emotional behaviour, to enable a firm to fully use its

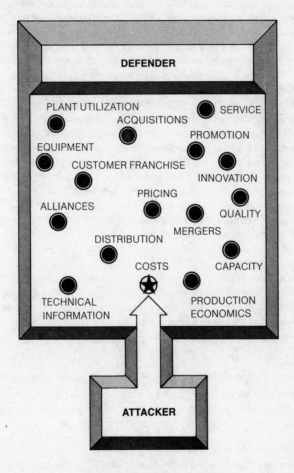

Figure 3.1
THE MINEFIELDS OF DETERRENCE

capabilities to deter a challenge. As the examples suggest, deterrent strategies are highly successful in avoiding fratricidal battles in the market, and provide companies with the ultimate victory of winning without resorting to a debilitating physical contest of resources. Military practitioners and theorists, from Sun Tzu around 500 BC through to the present day have believed implicitly in the strategic value of deterrence. Even Napoleon is quoted as stating that all his 'care will be to gain victory with the least shedding of blood'. Most deterrent strategies in business appear to be unconsciously adopted as part of the overall strategic response, rather than as a conscious competitive policy. Companies seem to be unable to resist the temptation of 'physical' conflict; they are wedded to the attack—defence syndrome, and forego the considerable benefits of deterrence. Since current market conditions favour innovative strategic approaches, those companies which actively pursue deterrent strategies have an opportunity to gain a high pay-off at the expense of competitors adopting the more traditional attack—defence responses to market conflict.

Source References

1. Forbes, September 28, 1981.

2. Financial Times, February 10, 1983.

3. Forbes, May 25, 1981 and The Economist, May 19, 1984.

4. Fortune, September 7, 1981.

5. The Wall Street Journal, March 24, 1981.

6. Business Week, January 26, 1981.

7. Forbes, March 2, 1982.

8. The Economist, November 6, 1982.

9. Fortune, July 27, 1981.

10. The Wall Street Journal, January 25, 1983.

11. The Economist, February 13, 1982.

12. The Economist, June 26, 1982.

13. Fortune, June 15, 1981.

14. The Economist, April 4, 1981.

15. Newsweek, March 4, 1983.

chapter four

OFFENCE

'In war, victory belongs to those who find in themselves the resolution to attack: those who are merely defensive are doomed to defeat'.

M. V. Frunze

The assault on an enemy is the classic offensive approach and is the most direct physical manœuvre used to challenge the status quo and upset the equilibrium in favour of the aggressor.

Companies and armies adopt five basic offensive manœuvres (see Table 4.1).

FRONTAL ATTACKS

'C'est magnifique, mais ce n'est pas la guerre!'

Attributed to General Bosquet (Balaclava, 1854)

The frontal attack is used to penetrate the centre of an enemy's position and is possibly the oldest offensive military manœuvre. However, a frontal attack is a direct assault upon an enemy and is the least desirable form of attack since attacks on well organized defensive systems are almost always destroyed. Some of the most spectacular successes and catastrophic failures on the battlefield have occurred as a result of frontal attacks.

El Alamein (1942), was a highly successful frontal attack. However, this assault was carried out with men, gun, tank and air superiority over the defenders of between 2 and 3 to 1 and with the reserves available to sustain a high level of casualties. Marlborough, while achieving spectacular successes with frontal attacks at Blenheim (1704) and Ramilles (1706), scored less impressive results at Malplaquet (1709), in the War of Spanish Succession. Marlborough's slight superiority in numbers did nothing to offset his losses of 2 to 1 to the Imperialists, and while he won the battle the

1.   FRONTAL ATTACKS

    – Success
    – Failure
    – Suicide

2.   FLANKING ATTACKS

    – Geographical
    – Marketing
    – Technology

3.   ENVELOPMENT

4.   ISOLATION

5.   UNCONVENTIONAL OFFENCE

    – Pricing
    – Promotion
    – Packaging
    – Products
    – Alliances
    – Executive Raiding
    – Legal Manœuvres
      Anti–Trust
      Patents
      Trade Restrictions
      Trademarks

Table 4.1
KEY OFFENSIVE STRATEGIES

engagement was probably the bloodiest in the 18th century. Classic failures of the frontal attack are almost too numerous to recount. In thirty minutes 500 out of 673 officers and troopers of the Light Brigade were killed, wounded or dehorsed in the suicidal frontal charge at Balaclava (1854). Even if the attacker has superior forces and can overwhelm the defenders, the losses may be unacceptable or the defence so spirited that the delay in penetrating the defences allows the enemy to regroup and resupply, providing only small gains for the successful attacker. The most disastrous use of frontal attacks was during the First World War (1914—1918). Both sides, wedded to the 'offence à l'outrance' concept advocated by du Picq and practised by Foch, Haig and Ludendorf, used massive frontal attacks in an attempt to break through the stalemate of trench warfare conditioned by the technological advance in defensive weaponry. The Somme offensive alone between July and November 1916 claimed over one and a quarter million casualties on both sides — slaughter on a scale never seen before or since; and the second battle of the Somme in March—April 1918 decimated a further 400,000 troops on both sides.

As in military combat, the frontal attack is a popular form of market assault with very similar outcomes.

Frontal attacks have been spectacular successes or catastrophic failures in business...

Successful Frontal Attacks

A frontal attack was launched by Casio, a small electronic watch manufacturer, on Citizen and Seiko who had revolutionized the watch industry with their skilful use of electronic technology and aggressive marketing. Casio used its extensive computer and consumer electronics know-how to drive the price of electronic quartz watches to new lows by marketing precision-made electronic time pieces complete with stop watch, alarm and time zone features for around $20. Casio's frontal attack had the potential of drawing Citizen and Seiko closer to the financial jungle inhabited by other consumer electronic products such as calculators where huge investments, rapid write-off and wafer thin margins are the rules for survival. In the face of Casio's successful attack both Citizen and Seiko repositioned themselves by all but abandoning the low cost segment of the electronic quartz watch market to Casio, concentrating on the mid-price range where they were less vulnerable to price attacks. By 1983, Casio had secured over 18% of the total Japanese watch market by operating only in the low cost segment and dominated Japanese digital display production.[1]

Airbus Industrie has achieved a significant position in the wide-bodied airliner market with a frontal attack against the dominant competitors, Boeing, Lockheed, and McDonnell-Douglas. Airbus Industrie, a consortium formed in 1970 by Aerospatiale (France) and Deutsche Airbus (Germany), was joined by Casa (Spain) in 1971 and BAC (UK) in 1979 and supported by two non-equity partners, Fokker (The Netherlands) and Belairbus (Belgium). The first product, the A300, which flew in October 1972 and went into service in 1974, was a twin-engine, twin aisle, 220—345 seater aircraft with a range of up to 4,000 miles. It utilized state-of-the-art technology, including a super critical wing which provided a low noise profile and significant fuel efficiency and gave a lower operating cost than competitive products. By using the European partners as captive markets for the essential launch orders and relying on multi-government finance, Airbus Industrie was able to use easy credit terms and penetration pricing policies to success-fully enter the world market for wide-bodied airliners. Airbus Industrie's strategy increased its market share from 3% in 1976 to 33% in 1981, and by mid-1983 Airbus Industrie had secured over 350 orders for the A300 and its line extension, the A310, from 46 airlines — over two-thirds of the orders from customers outside Europe and North America. Airbus Industrie's strategy was so successful that it virtually squeezed out Boeing and McDonnell-Douglas from that market segment in Africa, Asia, and the Middle East.[2]

IBM mounted a massive frontal assault on the $1.4 billion US personal computer market in August 1981 with its high priced PC model, designed to take leadership from the market creator and leader, Apple. IBM's corporate policy in entering the personal computer market was based on the belief that the personal computer was rapidly turning into the executive workstation, and the most popular method for business to tap into information processing at the desktop level. Unless IBM could attain a strong position in the personal computer market, it was believed that personal computers which could interface with mainframe and minicomputers could eventually threaten IBM's position in those

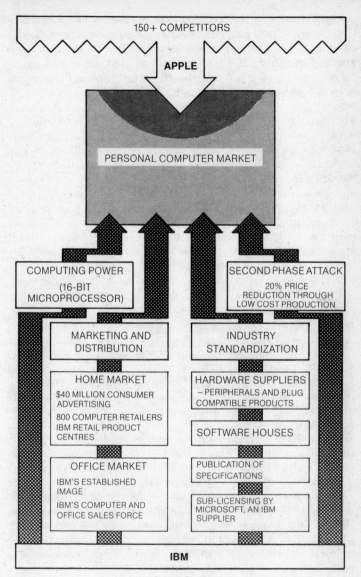

Figure 4.1
FRONTAL ATTACK
IBM's frontal attack on Apple's leadership in the US personal computer market.

markets. IBM's frontal attack on the market was based on a simultaneous three–pronged assault (see Figure 4.1). IBM's PC was designed around an Intel 16–bit microprocessor, providing much greater power than the majority of existing products which used 8–bit microprocessors, and this gave IBM an advantage in the office market. Secondly, IBM widely published its PC specifications and made them available to all software producers, and allowed Microsoft, the supplier of the PC's basic operating instructions, to license its software to other companies. The huge sales potential of IBM software created a major market as small software houses flocked to write IBM compatible software. This made IBM software the de facto personal computer industry standard in a previously unstandardized industry. Computer hardware companies also sensed the sales potential of the IBM PC and rapidly developed and marketed plug–compatible and peripheral products which re-inforced IBM's PC as the industry standard. IBM realized that marketing and distribution skills were more important than technology in the personal computer market. Shelf space in a market with over 150 competitors was a critical battle in the home computer segment, while in the office segment, companies pre-ferred to use products from established firms with developed after-sales service.

IBM attacked the home computer segment with a massive $40 million advertising campaign to attract customers who had not used a computer or heard of IBM. IBM used company–owned retail product centres and 800 carefully selected computer retailers to distribute the PC; while simultaneously using its huge sales force to penetrate the office segment, employing IBM's established credit-ability in the computer industry to sell the PC. By the end of 1982, IBM had secured a 17% share of the $24 million personal computer market, second to Apple.

IBM produced the PC using a large number of component manufacturers and assembled the product in highly automated factories to keep costs down. As a second phase in its offensive, IBM, using its cost advantages, reduced prices by 20% in April 1983, which sparked a round of industry price cutting as manufacturers attempted to remain competitive by offering higher performance at lower cost than the market leaders in order to maintain dealer interest and consumer attraction. The squeeze on margins produced a number of small company failures; those who were unable to compete with IBM's continued attack on the market. By concentrating on marketing and distribution skills, introducing standardization and ensuring low cost production with a product which was neither at the cutting-edge of personal computer technology or bargain priced, IBM had secured a dominant 26% share of the $4.2 billion US personal computer market by 1983 and displaced Apple as the market leader.[3]

In 1969 Philip Morris purchased the lacklustre Miller Brewing Company from W.R. Grace. Using packaged-goods marketing techniques new to the beer business, huge advertising budgets and ingenuity in developing low-calorie Lite Beer, Miller, through an aggressive frontal attack, was catapulted within four years from seventh to second place in the market, increasing its share from 4% to 24% and in the process rejuvenated the entire US brewing industry.[4]

While the Casio, Airbus Industrie, IBM and Philip Morris frontal attacks have been successful, a number of other frontal attacks on the market have not been as fortunate.

Unsuccessful Frontal Attacks

Continental Europe's largest English-language newspaper, the Paris-based International Herald Tribune (IHT), was at a distinct disadvantage to the British daily newspapers when the IHT was launched in the UK. The IHT was printed in Paris and airfreighted to the UK and arrived on the news-stands in the late morning. Since the cardinal rule in the newspaper market is that old news is no news, the IHT finally arranged with a UK-based printer, through facsimile transmission, to provide simultaneous printing of the same issue in London and Paris. Although this manœuvre enabled the IHT to reach the news-stands at the same time in the UK as the British dailies it was a pyrrhic victory since the IHT was unable to secure a significant market position due to its limited local news coverage and format.

The Financial Times, Europe's leading financial newspaper attempted to crack the US market with both its regular newspaper and special US weekly financial news magazine. The Financial

Times was printed in Frankfurt and airfreighted in the early hours of the morning to New York to enable the paper to be on the news-stands early in the morning to compete directly with the main competitor, the Wall Street Journal. The Financial Times also launched a special news magazine, World Business Weekly, in 1979 aimed at the US market. The Financial Times was not successful with either venture; while the newspaper continued to be air-freighted to New York, World Business Weekly was closed down in 1981 as losses were projected to run at over $1 million per annum with no break-even point in sight.[5]

Proctor & Gamble has consistently outspent (by 3 to 1) its arch rival Lever in promotion in the UK detergent market and has three brands, Ariel, Bold and Daz, to Lever's Persil and Surf. However, P&G has failed for 20 years to take market leadership from Lever. Lever's ability to gauge changing consumer preferences and needs has enabled Lever to maintain leadership in the detergent market despite P&G's promotional leverage. While Lever has lost market share, falling from 52% in 1961 to 40% in 1982, P&G also lost share dropping from 37% to 32% in the same time — as a result of competition from other brands rather than from eroding each others' market shares.

Other frontal attacks on the market-place have proved suicidal.

Suicidal Frontal Attacks

Rolls-Royce, facing a fall in sales due to slowing demand for military aero-engines and declining business for its older civil engines in the 1960s, decided to go for a big civil jet engine (RB 211). Rolls eventually found a US airframe manufacturer, Lockheed, to order the RB 211 to power the L1011, Tristar wide-bodied jet. Rolls signed a disastrous contract for an advanced technology engine incorporating radically new ideas such as carbon fibre hyfil blades in the fans. Rolls had no experience in this area and left insufficient margin for error. Early in 1971 Rolls-Royce went bankrupt, not because of the length and size of its order book, but due to the lack of sufficient cash flow to pay the bills.[6]

John Bloom initially enjoyed a phenomenal success with Rolls-Razor in the UK washing machine market in the late 1950s. Rolls-

Razor, a new competitor, outmanœuvred the market leaders, Hoover and Hotpoint, by using an aggressive door-to-door sales force working only on commission, supported by heavy advertising. Low costs in the form of imported parts and UK assembly, the absence of both retail margins and a high cost service-sales force enabled Bloom to price well below his competitors. By 1963, Rolls-Razor held a 20% market share and overtook Hotpoint and became the second leading brand. Rolls-Razor marketed two models, one at a loss and the other at a profit. Bloom geared production and marketing costs to sales; when overall volume declined substantially in 1964 and the sales unit mix changed from 5% in 1962 to 11% in 1964 in favour of the loss-making machine, Rolls-Razor's profits evaporated. By mid-1964 Rolls-Razor had gone into liquidation.

Freddie Laker, against intense opposition from IATA and individual airlines, started a highly successful low-priced trans-atlantic air service in 1977. During the five years of operation Laker Airways' Skytrain lured millions of customers away from traditional airlines with low prices and reached a new market segment — people who had never been able to afford transatlantic airfares. The combination of competitive response — a bewildering array of discount fares from major airlines which lost Laker its price advantage; the global recession — where passenger seat miles began to decline; currency fluctuations — where a 20% drop in the pound to dollar rate reduced passenger revenue and increased loan repayment charges; and bad management — where costs began to increase to a point where the airline's debt of £240 million could not be serviced; forced Laker into bankruptcy in February 1982.[7]

Rolls-Royce, Rolls-Razor and Laker Airways all made frontal attacks on markets where their resources were insufficient to meet and overcome either competitive reaction or a hostile environment. Novo Industri, on the other hand, realized that a frontal attack on the US insulin market with its novel monocomponent product against the market leader Eli Lilly with a 90% market share was, in the long term, suicidal. While Novo had achieved a respectable share of the US insulin market from its entry in the mid-1970s, the key to taking on Lilly was an alliance to gain a large-scale marketing resource. Novo formed a joint marketing venture in 1982 with E.R. Squibb which combined Novo's small but specialized marketing force with Squibb's much larger insulin-trained sales force forming an effective marketing alliance to fight Lilly.[8] By the end of 1983 the Novo–Squibb alliance had captured a 20% share of the US insulin market at the expense of Lilly.

The key to success in a frontal assault in both business and in war is to ensure that there are sufficient resources to overwhelm an opponent and to continue combat, and that the losses incurred are both predictable and can be sustained without devastating the organization. As the examples suggest, 'over–the–top' frontal attacks are high–risk manœuvres and there are no guarantees of success whatever the scale of resources used by an attacker. Other forms of assault, including flanking, envelopment, isolation, and unconventional offence, if skilfully employed can bring crushing defeats on competitors at lower risk and cost for the attacker.

FLANKING ATTACKS

'Flank attack is the essence of the whole history of warfare'.
Feldmarschall Alfred von Schlieffen

Flanking attacks are designed to pressure the flank of the enemy line in such a way as to turn and roll the flank of the line inwards towards the centre creating chaos.

Flanking attacks have been widely employed throughout military history. Frederick the Great, at Rossbach (1757), Wellington at Assaye (1803) in the British–Maratha War in India and von Moltke at Gravelotte (1870) in the Franco–Prussian War, all successfully used flanking attacks. In more modern times the amphibious landings by the Allies in Italy at Anzio (1944) some seventy miles behind German lines, and by the US 10th Corps in the Korean War at Inchon (1950) several hundred miles behind North Korean lines, are examples of successful flanking attacks.

Flanking Attacks in business exploit weaknesses in competitive defences by positioning strength against weakness in innovative ways and are mounted on geographical, marketing and technological thrusts.

Geographical Flanking

Geographical flanking attacks are made nationally and internationally in business conflict.

Delta Airlines successfully conducted a major flanking attack on rival airlines operating in the south-eastern United States. Delta perfected the 'hub and spoke' route system in which traffic from smaller towns are funnelled through the large airport at Atlanta where travellers changed flights for their ultimate destinations. Delta arranged its timetable so that ten times a day, 40 to 50 flights were on the ground simultaneously, ensuring that Delta passengers could interconnect with Delta flights with a minimum of delay providing a through service on Delta. Delta's flanking strategy was so successful that it outmanœuvred the larger Eastern as well as the smaller regional carriers like Ozark, Piedmont and Southern and secured the bulk of Atlanta transit passengers.[9]

Iowa Beef Processors geographically outflanked Swift Packing in the meat packing business using an innovative logistics strategy. Iowa built packing plants west of Chicago, on the plains near cattle feed-lots. Instead of shipping dressed carcasses it started carving the meat into chunks and shipping them in boxes, leaving only final slicing to the supermarkets. Iowa's strategy reduced shipping and labour costs and undercut Swift. Ironically, Iowa had taken Swift's original idea of dressing carcasses in Chicago, on which the company was founded in 1855, a stage further by locating nearer to the source of meat and providing greater benefits to the super-markets. Iowa's market position within a few years was such that the outflanked Swift attempted to sell off most of its fresh meat business in 1981.[10]

Outflanking competitors internationally is well illustrated by Dow Chemicals' thrust at the weakest flank of the PVC raw material market in Japan — the market for chlorine made through salt electrolysis which is combined with petrochemicals to make the building blocks for PVC. The Japanese chemical industry was fragmented, with 34 companies producing chlorine, and caustic soda as a co-product, in 53 plants with high raw material and energy costs (more than four times those of the USA). A Japanese government ruling in 1974 ordered the local chlorine-caustic soda industry to convert to a costly new technology after its use of mercury caused an environmental problem. Dow gambled on the probability that enough old Japanese capacity would be shut down to enable Dow to import a projected 600,000 tonnes of high margin chlorine a year by 1985.[11]

Marketing Flanking

Marketing flanking attacks are assaults exploiting demographic and behavioural factors which can be translated into market needs and which are either not being served by existing competitors or which are vulnerable to a concerted competitive assault.

De-regulation of the US airline industry in 1978 provided an opportunity for companies to enter previously protected enclaves in the airline market (see Figure 4.2). A number of small airlines were formed in the 1979—1981 period to fill profitable niches alongside existing airlines in the major high–density travel markets. Typical examples were Midway Airlines in Chicago (November 1979), New York Air in New York (December 1980) and People Express in Newark (April 1981). Although this strategy had been highly successful in intrastate air travel in California with PSA (1949) and Air California (1966), and in Texas with Southwest Airlines (1971), this was a new departure since it involved interstate rather than intrastate competition. The established carriers were highly vulnerable to aggressive price competition; they had accumulated layers of heavy costs dictated by labour agreements, large and expensive fuel–hungry jets which were costly to operate under conditions of rising fuel prices, and high cost services such as hot meals and luxurious terminals designed to attract passengers. By using a combination of tactics taking advantage of a surplus of low priced jet aircraft, using non–unionized labour from a surplus pool which had developed in the industry and eschewing passenger services, these small airlines were able to translate lower operating costs into low fares and drew business away from the established carriers. Midway in fact took advantage of the additional benefit of being able to fly from Cleveland, Detroit, Kansas City and New York into Midway airport in Chicago which is a few miles from the city centre, rather than O'Hare airport which was almost an hour commute from the centre of Chicago.[12]

During the 1960s, supermarket operators in the USA came to believe that 'Big is Beautiful' and that larger stores with massive car parking facilities were not only more attractive but more efficient to operate. As a result of this philosophy, the average supermarket size steadily increased. Convenience store operators defied the trend and introduced small stores, limited product selections, increased prices and worked longer hours. Convenience stores such as '7-

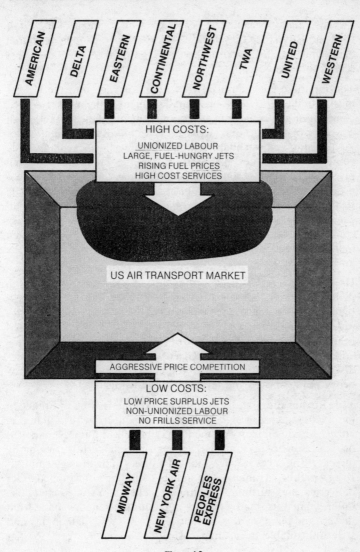

Figure 4.2
FLANKING ATTACK
New airlines, following de-regulation, which used cost as the basis for a flanking attack on established carriers in the US air transport market.

Eleven' quickly became the fastest growing segment of the retail food industry since they focused on special consumer needs not being met by the supermarkets and outflanked the larger less service-orientated outlets.[13]

The Japanese concentrated, from their entrance into the US car market in the early 1960s, on a small segment of the market — sub-compact cars — eschewing the major segments of the market which consisted of compact and large cars. After building a reputation for high quality and establishing a network of well-stocked and well-equipped dealers and service facilities, the Japanese were well placed to exploit, through a flanking attack, the opportunities presented after the two OPEC price increases in the mid and late 1970s. The major US companies had avoided the low profit small car segment of the market and had virtually no products in direct competition with Honda, Mazda, Nissan, Subaru and Toyota when market demand switched to sub-compact fuel-efficient cars in the late 1970s.

Hanes used classic packaged goods marketing techniques to revitalize the US market for womens' tights and in the process outflanked its much larger competitors. Hanes formulated its L'eggs product using memory yarn to provide a superior product, used innovative packaging in the form of a plastic egg to create an unique and visually appealing pack, and used new distribution channels — discount chains, drug stores and grocery outlets — supported by heavy point-of-sale and television advertising.[14]

Yves Rocher successfully introduced a cosmetics line in France in the 1960s against well-entrenched competitors with a flanking attack. Although luxury cosmetics had been traditionally marketed on a person-to-person basis, either through perfumeries or by direct selling, Yves Rocher adopted a direct mail strategy emphasizing a highly personalized approach, including gift wrapped order deliveries and birthday greetings to clients. Yves Rocher also differentiated its line by developing natural cosmetics made from flowers and plants to appeal to customers wanting high quality and style unavailable from other cosmetics companies. Yves Rocher rapidly established a high level of brand loyalty through its personalized promotion and differentiated products and became a leading factor in the French cosmetics market with orders growing from 162 million French francs in 1975 to 1.2 billion French francs in 1981.

Murjani of Hong Kong identified a trend towards dressier, more fashionable casual clothes in the mid-1970s and translated this into a new range of jeans using a celebrity, Gloria Vanderbilt, to promote the line as a high fashion item. The new 'designer' jeans were an immense success outflanking the market leaders Lee, Levi-Strauss and Wrangler who continued to promote lower margin down-market jeans. Murjani was rapidly followed by Calvin Klein, Jordache and Sasson and by 1981 designer jeans had created an entirely new market worth over $600 million in the US alone.

Technology Flanking

Outflanking competitors by a technological thrust aims at securing customers through an innovative benefit often based on a use or an application not immediately available to competitors.

Aerospatiale, the state-owned French helicopter manufacturer, is attempting to outflank the three largest free-world helicopter manufacturers — Bell Helicopter, Boeing and Sikorsky — by marketing technologically more advanced products. The huge military demand for helicopters in the Vietnam War kept the three American companies producing flat out and gave these firms little time for technological progress. Aerospatiale introduced simultaneously in 1980 three new generation fast twin-turbine models designed to cover all conceivable civilian and military needs. The models featured Aerospatiale-developed fail-safe rotor blades made from composite materials rather than conventional metal.[15]

Michelin, the tyre manufacturer used advanced technology to outflank its competitors in the USA. The bias- or cross-ply tyre had been around for decades and the major US tyre manufacturers invested minimal amounts in new technology, preferring to spend their resources on battles for market share. Michelin moved from an exporting base to local manufacture in the US in 1975 and supplied the specialist replacement tyre market with radial tyres. The major US manufacturers Goodrich, Goodyear, Firestone and Uniroyal concentrated efforts on the original equipment market where cross-ply tyres were sold for profit measured in pennies per tyre. This assured long production runs, kept brand names in front of consumers and set the stage for the lucrative replacement tyre market as cross-ply tyres wore out after 20,000 miles. During the late

1970s, the high cost of fuel resulted in consumers driving less, thus prolonging tyre life. The major US car manufacturers, to promote fuel-efficiency, switched to radial tyres as original equipment, which decreased fuel consumption by about 5%. Michelin aggressively pushed its way into the original equipment business and, sustaining its reputation for high quality, obtained an estimated 25% of the $4 billion US tyre market. The US manufacturers were caught by Michelin's technology flanking strategy since they lacked the manufacturing know-how to compete effectively with the radial tyre leader Michelin. Firestone's early counter-attack with its '500' series radial tyre failed due to quality deficiencies. The new technology brought additional problems. Radial tyres last for 40,000 miles, twice that of cross-ply tyres. With an average car life of 110,000 miles, this reduced (from 5 to 2) the opportunities to supply the lucrative replacement market. Shrinking demand for cross-ply tyres and fixed capacity led to cut-throat pricing and monumental inventory problems for those US tyre manufacturers who had continued to support the old technology.[16]

Tandem Computers outflanked the existing computer hardware manufacturers by producing a minicomputer designed for uninterrupted operation. The machine had a dual processor to provide a back-up processor if one failed, and the minicomputer could be serviced while operating flat out. Tandem machines sold rapidly to customers with specific reliability needs such as banks, continuous process factories, airlines and stock exchanges — segments of the minicomputer market where Tandem had an innovative advantage.[17]

Proctor & Gamble used technology to outflank Kimberley Clark and Scott Paper in the mature US paper-tissue market in the 1960s. Conventional market wisdom suggested that paper-tissue could be soft or strong but not both. P&G invested heavily in paper technology for over 5 years and developed a superior product which was both soft and strong. P&G's Charmin brand took the paper-tissue market by storm and left Kimberley Clark and Scott Paper with heavy investments in the old wet crepe paper technology which had been technologically outflanked by P&G.

The key to successful flanking attack in both war and business is to avoid weakening the centre to build up the required strength on the flank. In the battle of Austerlitz (1805) the Austrians and Russians weakened their centre on the Pratzen Heights to mass strength for a decisive strike against Napoleon's right flank. This provided Napoleon with the opportunity to deliver a counter-blow which sealed the Austrians' and Russians' fate. In business, there are similar examples. Air Florida's successful entrance into the domestic and international airline business was based on low-priced competition. The effects of these price wars came home to roost in the winter of 1981–1982. Air Florida was forced to redevelop local markets and find winter work for its four expensive long range DC-10 aircraft at a time when passenger traffic was falling and costs escalating as a result of poor economic conditions in the US. Air Florida attempted to build a series of intrastate and international routes based on Miami as the hub. However, new domestic routes to Dallas, Houston and Toledo, as part of the hub and spoke concept, and international routes to Amsterdam, Brussels, London and Shannon to feed traffic into Miami and to utilize its expensive DC-10 airliners failed, as the airline had no established image on which to build a local identity in these new non-Florida markets.[18] Following mounting losses in 1983 and early 1984 Air Florida ran into a liquidity problem and went bankrupt in June 1984.

In many respects flanking attacks are synonymous with segmentation where a firm uses geography, market conditions or technological product differentiation to separate the market and competitors into smaller, more manageable and more vulnerable segments.

ENVELOPMENT

'The deep envelopment based on surprise, which severs the enemy's supply lines, is and always has been the most decisive manœuvre of war'.

General Douglas MacArthur (1950)

Envelopment is the complete encirclement of the enemy's force on both flanks and is designed to force an enemy to capitulate or face deprivation or annihilation.

Encirclement has been used as a strategy to win by avoiding serious fighting. Oliver Cromwell at Preston (1648), Napoleon at Ulm (1805), von Moltke at Sedan (1870) and Allenby in Sumaria (1918) are examples of the successful use of encirclement which minimized the use of force. The outcomes of some encirclements are so decisive that they can be considered turning points in conflicts. For example Yorktown (1781) in the American War of Independence, Port Arthur (1905) in the Russo–Japanese War, and Dien Bien Phu (1954) all resulted in decisive victories which sealed the fate of both the encircled army and the overall conflict.

In a business context, encirclement has been a successful offensive strategy.

Boeing adopted an envelopment strategy by developing a family of jet airliners to offer a full product range (see Figure 4.3). The original 707–120 was essentially a domestic model which was supported by the –300 and –400 series intercontinental models. These were to compete with the Comet 4 and the Douglas DC–8 while the 720, a special short–haul, short–fuselage lightweight transcontinental version, was developed to combat the Comet 3 and Convair 880. These models were supplemented by the tri–jet 727 model, a medium range jet which eventually became the world's largest selling jet airliner. This was followed by the short range 737 to compete primarily with Douglas' DC–9 and the BAC One–Eleven, and the 747 'jumbo jet', a mass–transport intercontinental jet. To complete the envelopment of competitive products the basic 727 and 737 models were lengthened (–200 series) and the 747 was offered in a special short–body form (747 SP) for long range lower density routes and a model with an extended upper–deck (747–300SUD) to increase carrying capacity. Despite heavy competition, by 1980 Boeing was taking almost two of every three civil jets ordered world–wide as a result of a family of products covering a range of market segments.[19]

Visa achieved its major position in the bank credit card business by a series of innovative product and service strategies. These were designed to develop the market by putting together an infrastructure to aid and extend the credit cards offered by banks supporting Visa which would envelop their competitors. Visa developed the first computerized system for the electronic transfer of data between banks and pioneered an international magnetic strip for the bank card. They were also the first to combine international institutions under a common name for the marketing of financial services and to develop a 'debit' card that could directly tap deposit accounts.[20]

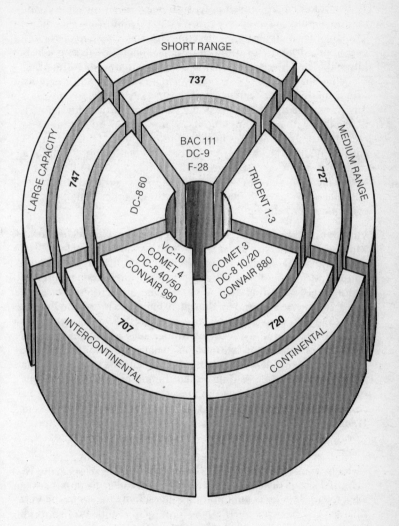

Figure 4.3
ENVELOPMENT
Boeing Airplane Company's encirclement of the civil jet airline market and of competitive products.

Tandy adopted an envelopment strategy in its attack on the microcomputer market. One model was aimed at the major segment, the small business operator. This was essentially a refined and updated model of Tandy's original machine offering a 16K internal memory, a disc drive to provide adequate data storage and a custom-made desk. The second model was a hand-held computer with a small memory, a typewriter-format keyboard and a display; this was targeted at the professional worker and priced low enough to compete with programmable calculators. The third machine was aimed primarily at the home market and schools. Tandy's envelopment strategy was enhanced by marketing the microcomputer range through its own Radio Shack outlets. This technique avoided the drain on margins suffered by other manufacturers and offered the opportunity for a sustained and controlled marketing effort.[21]

Vlasic Foods, a regional company enveloped the US pickle market with an innovative strategy in the 1970s. The market in the late 1960s was dominated by a few national, standardized, brands from Heinz and Del Monte, and by a large number of local brands tailored to regional tastes selling in major population centres. Vlasic, a successful regional brand in Detroit, began to acquire local brands across the US but astutely maintained each brands' characteristics to maintain a franchise with consumers. As Vlasic extended its coverage of the US it began to use national TV and in-store promotion to fuel demand. By the end of the 1970s, Vlasic, through its acquisition policy, had encircled the market, by providing the resources for national promotion together with the advantages of a consumer-tailored product and low, localized, distribution costs. Heinz, once the market leader, saw its share of the pickle market fall to 10% as Vlasic's envelopment strategy enabled the company to attain a 26% market share.[22]

In both military and business combat the success of an encirclement strategy is dependent on the superiority of force or resources used to envelop the enemy. If these forces are inadequate, the unit runs the risk of being over-extended and of facing a break-out by the enemy using superior forces against the unit's weakest point. One of the greatest military encirclement failures occurred in Normandy in 1944. Patton's Third Army pushed two German armies against Montgomery's 21st Army group at Falaise. Problems with command structures, communications and misunderstanding enabled the majority of German troops to escape through a gap between the two allied armies. The failure to close the Falaise gap was one of the greatest tactical failures of World War II and one which could have shortened that war had it been successful.

Encirclement failures have also occurred in business conflict. Exxon's attempted ten year encirclement of the office automation business and the two major combatants — IBM and Xerox — was a classic encirclement failure. Exxon purchased a range of companies to provide the products to envelop the office automation market and the competition. Danbury Systems (high resolution ink-jet computer printers), Delphi Communications (computer and telephone answering systems), Intecon (digital switching networks), Kylex (flat panel computer display screens), Optical Information Systems (semi-conductor lasers), Periphonics (computer voice response systems), QYX(electronic typewriters),QWIP (facsimile machines), Ramtek (computer terminals), Star Systems (optical disk memory systems), Vydek (word processors), Xonex (advanced workstations) and Zilog (microprocessors) were all purchased as part of the encirclement campaign. Ineffective consolidation of the various independent entrepreneurial businesses, incompatible products and the lack of successful product replacement strategies throughout the Exxon Enterprises Group because of both a policy of selling what they had (which was rarely better than competing products) rather than waiting for products still being developed, and the rapid replacement of top management, all resulted in a staggering loss in 1980 of $150 million on sales of $270 million.[23]

ISOLATION

'This was the type of strategy we hated most. The Americans attacked and seized, with minimum losses, a relatively weak area, constructed airfields, and then proceeded to cut the supply lines. Our strong points were gradually starved out....... The Americans flowed into our weaker points and submerged us, just as water seeks the weakest entry to sink a ship'.

General Matsuichi Ino.

The key to position defence strategies are fortified strong points and trenches designed to break up offensive frontal attacks. The counter to position defence is an isolation strategy where strong points are bypassed by the main forces and mopped up by later waves of troops or left to surrender.

Isolation strategies are used to avoid bloody, frontal confrontations, particularly those which would cause unacceptable levels of casualties or blunt the offensive by bogging down large numbers of troops for long periods of time in siege situations. The Allied offensive strategy in the Pacific in World War II was to work towards a position within air and sea striking distance of Japan, leap–frogging across the ocean by a series of amphibious landings, and bypassing numerous Japanese island strongholds, whose garrisons soon became as useless as if they had been in prisoner–of–war camps. The capture of Okinawa (June 1945) gave the Allies an airbase for the final assault on Japan and cut sea communications to all southerly Japanese positions thereby isolating the Japanese positions in Burma, China, the Dutch East Indies and Malaya.

In the market–place, isolation strategies are used in a manner similar to that of battlefield combat — to avoid bloody confrontations where the challenger could stand to lose more than the defender in a frontal attack.

In the early 1970s, Bell's Scotch whisky was just another brand in the United Kingdom. Bell could not match the high advertising and promotion levels of the major brands in a frontal attack and therefore adopted an isolation strategy focusing on limited advertising designed to promote the use of mixers with Scotch whisky, and on distribution. The promotional campaign raised the number of women whisky drinkers, most of whom use mixers, to 40% of the total. At the same time Bell built its own sales network which called on both independent and brewery–controlled public houses; the latter being competitors, since several breweries also owned major brands of Scotch whisky. The Bell sales force was highly effective with hard sell tactics, and the orders for Bell's whisky increased so significantly that brewers were forced to buy from Bell or starve on lost commission. Bell's revenues increased by 800% from 1970 to 1979 and Bell's whisky became UK brand leader through its   isolation   strategy which bypassed the distribution system and focused on a specific customer niche.[34]

Sturm Ruger, a small US gun manufacturer, realized in the early 1950s that it could not compete with the large gunmakers such as

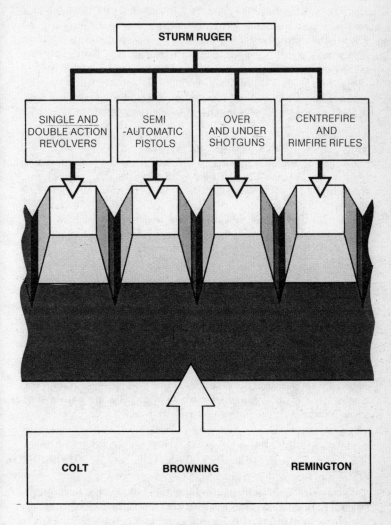

Figure 4.4
ISOLATION STRATEGY
Sturm Ruger's bypass strategy isolating Colt, Browning and Remington in the US sporting
guns market.

Browning, Colt and Remington in all product lines since the company did not have the capital to develop and produce a full line. Sturm Ruger adopted a bypass strategy by concentrating on producing competitively priced, high quality individual weapons that would clearly be the best in their class (see Figure 4.4). By adopting an isolation strategy focusing on quality and a limited range, Sturm Ruger had found enough niches over thirty years to secure almost 20% of the $350 million US domestic sporting guns market and isolate its competitors to the remainder.[25]

The market for zip fasteners in the US was once dominated by Talon. YKK, a newcomer to the market, realized that any attempt to secure a share of the market would face formidable competition from Talon. YKK isolated Talon by turning the lowly zip fastener into a high fashion item and selling direct to fashion design houses; this bypassed Talon's lock on the traditional distribution system — the wholesale network. Within a few years YKK obtained a 30% share of the US market at the expense of Talon. YKK repeated this successful isolation strategy in Europe and has achieved market leadership with a share of 28—30% of the world market through its forty local manufacturing plants and 100 sales offices in 39-countries which generated $916 million in sales in 1983.[26]

Monarch Wine, a small US firm with $60 million sales, acquired the US distribution rights to Tsingtao beer from mainland China in 1978. Monarch did not have the funds to mount a national promotion and distribution campaign and used an isolation strategy bypassing the normal channels of distribution for beer. Monarch focused only on the 12,000 licensed Chinese restaurants in the US and soon gained almost total distribution with a steep growth in sales through its unique position as the sole Chinese beer available in Chinese restaurants. Monarch's approach was so successful that within a few years Tsingtao had become a major force in the US imported beer market solely as the result of an isolation strategy.[27]

Isolation strategies in business share many of the characteristics of market segmentation, but they differ in that they are niche strategies which try to avoid provoking a massive competitive retaliation by evoking emotional responses as would a segmentation attack. Bang & Olufsen, a small Danish manufacturer of hi-fi and television equipment, has isolated and secured an exclusive, and highly profitable, niche representing less than 2% of the European market. B&O has focused on high quality, very stylish, easy to operate equipment at premium prices, sometimes as much as 20% over comparable products. Using largely word–of–mouth advertising and selling mood and style in high priced state–of–the–art equipment, B&O has avoided the traditional hi–fi enthusiasts' market and created a special niche which is too small in volume and profits to either attract or threaten the likes of Grundig, Philips, Sony and Panasonic.

UNCONVENTIONAL OFFENCE

'The enemy advances, we retreat.
The enemy encamps, we harass.
The enemy retreats, we pursue'.

Mao Zedong.

Unconventional offence, or guerrilla warfare, is a form of combat adopted by irregular forces fighting small scale, limited actions, against orthodox military forces.

In its basic form it is fighting in defence of home and country and is a method of protest against wrongs committed by an invader or a ruler. Most of the great conquests of history include guerrilla actions — Darius, Alexander and Hannibal all fought against guerrillas and the Romans fought guerrilla warfare for over two hundred years in Spain before the birth of Christ. Over time guerrilla warfare became an adjunct to political–military strategy where it complemented orthodox operations. Classic examples include the War of Independence (1775—1783) where irregulars helped to drive Cornwallis from the Carolinas to defeat at Yorktown (1781); and Yugoslavia (1941—1945), where Tito successfully tied down major German troop concentrations. Guerrilla tactics have also been used in an aggressive role, for example by the Goths and Huns, who began the destruction of the Western Roman Empire; the Vikings, who overran Britain and France; and the Mongols who cut a swath from Asia through to central Europe. The key objective of all forms of unconventional offence is to create both a physical and a morale situation where the instigator can secure concessions from the invader or ruler.

In business, unconventional offence is used as a prime combat strategy in an aggressive role to harass competitors to the extent that a firm can win concessions in the form of increased market share. Unconventional offensives take a number of forms in business conflict (see Figure 4.5).

PRICING — selective price attacks.
Boots introduced its Rufen brand of ibuprofen, an anti-arthritic drug, in the US in the Autumn of 1981. Boots, which had licensed ibuprofen, (marketed as Motrin), to Upjohn in 1974 adopted a radical penetration pricing strategy to secure market share. Boots offered Rufen at a 20% discount under Motrin's price plus $1.50 rebate to patients each time they purchased a 100 tablet bottle of Rufen — a move unheard of in the marketing of prescription drugs. Since the government Medicare and Medicaid programmes would only reimburse pharmacists for the lowest cost drug, Boots stood to gain the estimated 20% of sales of Motrin delivered under the Medicare/Medicaid programmes. Since a large number of arthritis sufferers are in the older age groups, many retired and on fixed incomes, Boots' pricing strategy provided the opportunity for Rufen to reach a large number of additional price-sensitive consumers.[28]

PROMOTION — product comparisons.
Flymo and Qualcast, each with around a third of the UK powered-lawnmower market, conducted aggressive promotional campaigns in 1980 and 1981 berating each others products[29] As part of Coca-Cola's 1979 attack on the US wine market Coca-Cola repositioned Taylor Wine as a Californian wine using a series of controversial taste-test comparisons claiming that a panel of experts preferred Taylor wine to those of old line Californian competitors such as Almadén, Ingelnook and Sebastiani.[30]

PACKAGING — locking-out competitors.
In the US, Wyeth developed and widely marketed the Tubex system for injectable applications in hospitals and provided a line of antibiotic and analgesic drugs to complement the system. To convert from the Tubex system hospitals would face the write-off of existing Tubex equipment and the purchase of a new system.

PRODUCTS — offering innovative alternatives.

Rent-a-Wreck has built a network of 250 car hire outlets in the US and a turnover (in 1982) of $30 million a year by renting old cars, some as much as 30 years old. With low costs, because wrecks do not depreciate and are inexpensive to buy, Rent-a-Wreck has been able

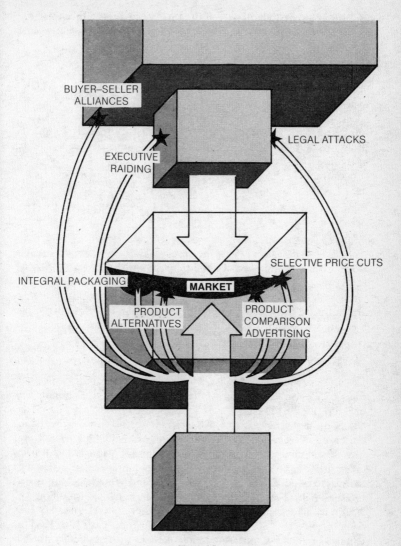

Figure 4.5
UNCONVENTIONAL OFFENCE
Guerrilla tactics used in conjunction with a conventional frontal attack to weaken
competitors.

to charge about half the price of Avis and Hertz, and while the giants have encountered falling demand and lower profits, Rent-a-Wreck's profits have doubled in each of the past five years.[31]

ALLIANCES

Osborne Computers used distributor and supplier alliances which, to the computer market, were innovative in scope and depth, to successfully launch the Osborne portable computer. Special deals were struck with software publishers to distribute their complete programs for the Osborne machine at nominal rates which overcame the need to hire a staff of programmers. Osborne subcontracted everything to keep prices down and made extensive use of volume to cut costs even further. By having suppliers hold inventory and with a low labour component the Osborne was introduced successfully at a price 40—60% less than comparable systems.[32]

EXECUTIVE RAIDING — hiring 'away' talent.

Coca-Cola strengthened its Wine Spectrum division in 1979 by hiring two sales managers from its leading US competitors, E & J Gallo and United Vintners[33] Among the computer, semiconductor and software companies in the Bay area of San Francisco, raiding has almost become institutionalized with a staff turnover in the region of 24% in 1982.

LEGAL MANŒUVRES

Anti-Trust Violations. MCI, a small telephone company with 1980 sales of $205 million, successfully attacked AT&T's monopoly on the lucrative US long-distance telephone call market. MCI based its attack on using new microwave technology and low overheads to undercut AT&T's long-distance charges. MCI began selling business clients its telephone service between a few heavy traffic cities in 1972, beaming calls by microwave and then transferring calls to local AT&T phone lines to reach individual customers. In 1969 and 1971 the Federal Communications Commission in landmark decisions allowed MCI and other competitors to break AT&T's 50-year monopoly on long-distance calls. In 1980 a Chicago Federal Court ruled that AT&T, with revenues of $50 billion, had to pay MCI $1.8 billion in damages for failing to let MCI use AT&T's local landlines to relay calls between 1971 and 1975. MCI's award was the largest antitrust settlement in US history.[34]

Patent Violations. Mistral, a Swiss-based manufacturer of wind-surfing boards lost an important patent infringement suit to the US originator, Windsurfer, in 1980 when it attempted to crack the West Germany market. Mistral got around Windsurfers' patent and the West German restraining order by selling the surfboard and sail separately.[35]

Import Violations. To avoid paying US import duty of 25% on completed trucks, Nissan and Toyota shipped truck cabs and chassis separately from Japan to the US and bolted them together locally and paid only 4% duty as imported parts. To counter this cost advantage Volkswagen, which had invested in a large production facility in the US, was successful in getting the US Customs Service to reclassify the Nissan and Toyota products as complete trucks and thereby incur the full 25% duty.[36]

Trademark Violations. In the UK, ICI was successful in preventing both the infringement of copyright and imitation of the appearance of its Inderal product — the world's largest selling betablocker drug — by a UK pharmacy.[37] It was also successful in preventing another company, Berk, from using the same dosage, biconvex shape, carmine colour and identical score marks on its Berkolol, a branded generic version of Inderal.[38]

Unconventional warfare in business differs from the military in degree rather than in kind. Unconventional tactics in business are constrained by the reality of moves that can be undertaken while in warfare almost anything goes.

Guerrilla warfare is an extreme form of unconventional offence using illegal methods such as pirating copyrights, patents and trademarks to produce counterfeit products. Computers, drugs, cosmetics, gramophone records, designer jeans, videotapes and many other products have fallen victim to guerrilla warfare. While counterfeiting can be contained by legal measures in most of the industrialized countries, companies have little chance of combating guerrilla warfare in some parts of Europe, Latin America and South-East Asia, where counterfeiting is largely concentrated, because of lax legal controls and the mobility of small pirate producers. Counterfeiting is now a world-wide problem thought to be worth $40 billion a year, or 2% of world trade. As the scale of pirating has grown so have the costs of containment. Vuitton, the french maker of luxury luggage spends up to $1 million a year to combat product piracy.[39]

In war most unconventional conflict is conducted by small groups against a larger enemy, primarily as the small group lacks the resources to mount effective conventional attacks. Despite the lack of resources, unconventional warfare can be extremely successful in changing policies. The object of the Second Seminole War (1835—1842) was to rid Florida of the Seminole Indians. The Indians, with a force never exceeding 1,000 warriors and with no industrial base, no outside help and no arms except those they possessed or captured, tied down 10,000 regular soldiers and 30,000 volunteers for seven years before the US government left them in possession of a large tract of land in Florida. In contrast, in market combat, as the examples show, unconventional tactics are used by companies of all sizes to further their aims. Unconventional offensives in both military and business combat are invariably resource intensive. They either form the major offensive strategy for small groups or firms challenging the status quo or are an integral component of an overall military or business strategy.

In military and business conflict, unconventional offence has been a highly successful form of combat since it is a flexible form of warfare which is difficult to effectively counter in a short time–scale frame given the static battlefield and market stance of most armies and companies. Thayer aptly remarked, 'Guerrillas never win wars, but their adversaries often lose them'.

SUMMARY

Attack is widely regarded as the most effective form of combat as it provides the aggressor in both war and business with a key ingredient for success — the initiative. Patton believed, for example, that 'the way to prevent the enemy from attacking you is to attack him and keep right on attacking him'. The successful attack whether using frontal, flank, encirclement, isolation or unconventional offence or their combinations depends on the careful selection of the objective, the enemy and the battlefield. Underestimating the enemy and the battlefield and overestimating the value of the objective have led to debacles in offensive strategies.

The Argentines, in occupying the Falkland Islands in 1982,

underestimated the morale, capabilities, training and resolve of the British to regain the islands. Similarly Polaroid's string of market failures in the late 1970s and early 1980s were based on an underestimation of competition and the market-place. Polaroid misjudged the home-movie market when it introduced Polavision, a high cost instant movie system in 1977, at a time when the more flexible portable video-recorders were being launched. The highly priced product which cost between $200 and $500 million in R&D and production charges to bring to market was withdrawn in 1980. Polaroid also misjudged the rise of the 35mm single lens reflex camera, which became simpler to operate and less expensive to buy, and underestimated the technical capabilities of Kodak which introduced an interchangeable-lens instant camera and film in 1981 in direct competition with Polaroid's main product line.[40]

As in war, attack in the market-place may not always be the most profitable strategy. Unfortunately both armies and companies are prone to adopt the disastrous offence á l'outrance — the blind doctrine of attack at any cost. While attack is often quoted as the best form of defence, decisive results can be attained only if the firm has the resources and the resolve to mount an effective offensive and can outperform its rivals and is fully aware of the competitors' defence and market conditions.

Source References

1.   The Economist, August 16, 1980.

2.   The Economist, August 27, 1983.

3.   Business Week, October 3, 1983.

4.   Fortune, June 29, 1981.

5.   The Economist, October 10, 1982.

6.   New Scientist, May 21, 1981.

7.   Newsweek, February 15, 1982.

8.   Financial Times, March 16, 1982.

9.   The Economist, September 26, 1981.

10.   The Wall Street Journal, February 5, 1981.

11.   The Economist, February 7, 1981.

12.   Fortune, February 9, 1981.

13.   Management Review, March, 1980.

14.   McKinsey Quarterly, Summer, 1982.

15.   The Economist, January 31, 1981.

16.   Fortune, October 20, 1980.

17.   The Economist, February 14, 1981.

18.   Business Week, April 19, 1982.

19.   The Economist, February 14, 1980.

20.   Business Week, December 22, 1980.

21.   The Economist, August 9, 1980.

22.   McKinsey Quarterly, Spring, 1981.

23.   Business Week, August 24, 1981.

24.   Business Week, December 6, 1982.

25.   Forbes, March 2, 1981.

26.   McKinsey Quarterly, Spring, 1981 and International Management, December, 1983.

27.   Forbes, September 28, 1981.

28.   The Wall Street Journal, September 23, 1981.

29.   The Financial Times, September 14, 1981.

30.   Business Week, October 15, 1979.

31.   The Economist, September 11, 1982.

32.   Fortune, March 8, 1982.

33.   Business Week, October 15, 1979.

34.   Time, February 23, 1981.

35.   The Economist, February 14, 1981.

36.   The Economist, November 8, 1980.

37.   IMS Monitor (Europe), January, 1980.

38.   Pharmaceutical Technology, August, 1980.

39.   Time, May 28, 1984.

40.   Business Week, March 2, 1981.

chapter five

DEFENCE

'Defence is the stronger form of war'.

Carl von Clausewitz.

Defensive strategies are combat manœuvres used to resist an attack and to inflict such losses on an attacker that he will either retreat or provide the defender with an opportunity to take the initiative and counter-attack.

In war and business conflict armies and companies use six basic defensive manœuvres (see Table 5.1).

POSITION DEFENCE

'Ils ne passeront pas!'.

Marshall Henri Pétain (Verdun 1916).

Position or point defence is the protection of fortified positions. In a strategic context cities and military installations and positions which command the approaches to an enemy target such as hilltops, mountain ridges and water crossings are representative of position defences.

Before the introduction of field artillery, position defences were subject to siege tactics where the aggressor attempted to starve out the defenders by denying resupply. The success of position defences under siege depends on the strength of the defence, the available supplies and the resolve of the aggressor. Through the Middle Ages, sieges frequently lasted from months to years and military operations in the seventeenth century were dominated by siege warfare. The period 1618—1722 saw over 120 major sieges, most taking place during the War of Spanish Succession. The advent of artillery, explosives and later, air power, have reduced the value of position defence as a major strategy; however, despite these counter

1. POSITION DEFENCE

- Differentiation
- Cost
- Promotion
- Resources
- Line Extensions
- Ownership

2. MOBILE DEFENCE

3. PRE-EMPTIVE STRIKE

- Resource Strikes
- Technology Strikes
- Market Strikes
- Financial Strikes
- Customer Strikes
- Distribution Strikes
- Political Strikes

4. FLANK POSITIONING

- Market Repositioning
- Resource Repositioning

5. COUNTER OFFENSIVE

- Product Counter Offensive
- Promotional Counter Offensive
- Production Counter Offensive
- Financial Counter Offensive
- Alliance Counter Offensive
- Combination Counter Offensive

6. STRATEGIC WITHDRAWAL

- Product Failure
- Social Withdrawal
- Technological Withdrawal
- Political Withdrawal

Table 5.1
KEY DEFENSIVE STRATEGIES

weapons not all modern sieges have been successful. Leningrad was besieged for 900 days (1941—1944) and although the defenders suffered appalling losses the city was never taken. Similarly while the isolated US Marine outpost at Khe Sanh was besieged by numerically superior Viet-Cong and North Vietnamese forces in 1968, the position was not breached. Although there has been strong military precedents over time which oppose a strategy based on the use of fixed fortified positions, these lessons have not always been observed. The Hindenburg Line was shattered in a matter of months by combined British, French and US attacks in 1918; the Maginot Line was bypassed by the Wehrmacht in 1940 in a week; and the Israeli Bar-Lev Line was breached by the Egyptians in a few days in the Yom Kippur War of 1973.

Position defence in business conflict involves the erection of fortifications, or barriers to entry, around a product, service or the company to protect against competitive aggression (see Figure 5.1). A number of sub-strategies are used in business to defend market positions.

Differentiation

The creation of unique features to distinguish a product from the competition is a key position defence manœuvre designed to protect the product's customer franchise. The perception of the product created by the differentiation can be such that the unique features not only insulate the product from a competitive challenge but also create such brand loyalty that a level of price insensitivity develops in consumers enabling higher margins to be charged. Product differentiation can take many forms;

CUSTOMER SERVICE

A key feature of Scandinavian Airline Systems' (SAS) successful defensive strategy in late 1981 was the reorientation of the airline from a production to a service enterprise. The increase in the quality and quantity of customer service in the air and on the ground was a major contributor to SAS' successful reversal of the airline's decline in Scandinavian and international market share.[1]

Cray has cornered the market for specialized supercomputers used by the military and scientists for fast number-crunching by virtually hand building its computers to customer specifications. This has provided Cray with a reservoir of customer loyalty which

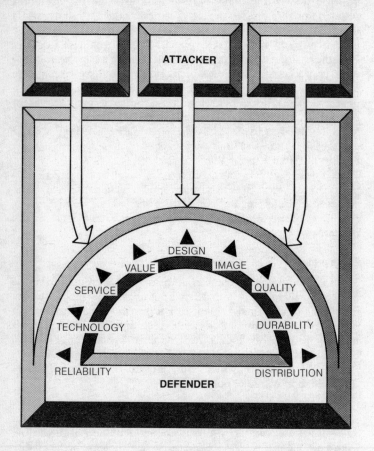

Figure 5.1
POSITION DEFENCE
Differentiation used as a defensive barrier to fight off competitive attacks.

no other company has been able to emulate and secured Cray's exclusive hold in the super-computer segment of the mainframe market.

DESIGN

Braun, a West German consumer electonics manufacturer, and Zenith, a Swiss watchmaker, have both secured valuable market niches by attracting and keeping customers through the innovative use of product design to differentiate their products. The designs are of such high standard that both firms have products on permanent display at the Museum of Modern Art in New York.

DISTRIBUTION

Heineken's maintenance of its commanding 40% share of the US imported beer market has largely been achieved through its national distribution system which no other imported beer has been able to emulate. Heineken is available almost everywhere in the US and can be purchased in 70% of all retail outlets handling alcoholic beverages. The wide distribution leads to fast turnover which ensures fresh beer and reinforces Heineken's quality image.[2]

DURABILITY

Land Rover, the utilitarian four-wheel drive vehicle conceived in the UK in the late 1940s, has outsold all other professional cross-country vehicles in Africa, Asia, Latin America and the Middle East for 40 years despite greater passenger comfort and more modern design offered by competitive products. Land Rover's proven record of durability in tough conditions over long periods of time is more important to customers in the bush, desert, forest and mountains than are electronic gadgets and creature comforts in vehicles which rapidly wear out.

EXCLUSIVITY

By limiting production and maintaining high quality and by selling through a few controlled retail outlets at high prices, Rolex has managed to maintain its up-market position in the highly volatile watch market. Although the market demands high levels of accuracy of within 15 seconds a month even for disposable low-cost quartz watches, Rolex, through its cultivated aura of exclusivity, has been able to steadily increase sales, to an estimated $350 million in 1983, of its mechanical chronometers which, though precision-made, can only maintain accuracy to within six seconds *a day*.

Rolex' exclusivity was sufficient to differentiate its products and avoid the 'Waterloo' experienced by other Swiss watch manufacturers faced with competition from low–cost, precision, electronic watches from Japan, Hong Kong, and Taiwan in the 1970s.

IMAGE

Hewlett–Packard was able to successfully avoid the cut–throat price war and the fate of many of its competitors in the personal calculator market in the mid–1970s by using its respected corporate image as a high quality advanced technology company to carve out and dominate a profitable niche in the market for personal high-priced, high–performance, business and scientific calculators.

PACKAGING

In the UK retail wine market, packaging has assumed a major role in product differentiation. Stowells' wine in a plastic lined bag, shapely glass jars by Grants of St. James', and wine in cans by Justerini & Brooks for their La Sonnelle range have all secured significant market positions through their innovative uses of packaging which have proved formidable defences against new competitors using the more traditional bottles to market wine.

QUALITY

Through skilful public relations and consumer promotion Honda has been able to secure and defend a strong position in the US small car market at much higher margins than all of its competitors by creating and maintaining the perception of high quality through superior fit and finish of its Acclaim, Accord, Civic and Prelude range of cars.

RELIABILITY

Tandem Computers' innovative use of a dual processor in its minicomputer offered uninterrupted operation, with a back–up if one processor failed, and servicing while operating flat-out. Tandem has never been successfully challenged in markets where customers have specific reliability needs such as airlines, banks, continuous process factories and stock exchanges.[3]

TASTE

Bailey's Original Irish Cream's unique blend has created a special taste which its myriad of later competitors have been unable to emulate. The distinctive taste advantage of the innovator has enabled Bailey's to maintain leadership at premium prices while many of its competitors have been forced to discount to stay in the market.

TECHNOLOGY

Michelin's continuous dedication to developing proprietary radial tyre technology has enabled the company to maintain its leading position world-wide in the radial tyre market at superior margins despite concerted attacks from its competitors.[4]

VALUE

Although the British Home Stores and Littlewoods mini-department stores have the same quality and assortment of private label goods available at lower prices, they have never been able to mount a successful challenge to Marks & Spencer, the UK retail private label market leader. Marks & Spencer has been able to create and maintain a value-for-money image which has become virtually unassailable by its competitors.

Cost

By achieving the lowest delivered cost position relative to competition firms can build strong position defences since the lowest costs provide the highest margins. High margins also present additional ammunition for further cost, price or promotional battles which higher cost competitors are unable to match without weakening their own profit positions. Cost leadership requires sub-strategies which emphasize the development of large economies of scale in purchasing, manufacturing, selling, distributing, promoting and servicing using cumulative experience and increases in efficiency and volume to drive costs down. These costs are further contained through vigorous attention to overheads and capital expenditure. A number of companies have successfully used the lowest delivered cost position as a key position defence strategy to combat challenges to their market leadership.

Electrolux, the Swedish consumer durables manufacturer, identified that market leadership in its slowly growing markets was dependent on low unit costs rather than on brand differences. By aggressively keeping its unit costs lower than competitors, Electrolux has achieved and maintained a 25% share of the world market for vacuum cleaners, somewhat more than Hoover's share. Hoover has a market share bigger than Electrolux only in the UK and USA.[5]

Texas Instruments (TI) used its leverage as the leader in new solid-state technology in the early 1970s to bring personal calculator production costs progressively lower. Lower costs provided opportunities to price lower which in turn opened up successively larger volume market segments which increased demand, again forcing costs down. TI's success with the Experience Curve Strategy (see Chapter 8) in achieving the lowest delivered cost position was such that by 1977 TI had gained market leadership in the personal calculator market — a position it still held until the early 1980s by maintaining its cost leadership strategy.[6] While there are a number of other examples of successful cost leadership in manufactured products — Briggs and Stratton in fractional horsepower motors and Swedish Match in disposable cigarette lighters are typical — cost leadership can provide position defence in other businesses. Electronic consumer goods retailers such as 47th Street Photo in New York, Comet in the UK and Eschen-Moser in Switzerland; Federal Express in the US air courier market; and People Express in the US regional airline business have all secured strong shares and contained competitive threats by achieving the lowest delivered cost position relative to competition.

Promotion

A well accepted maxim in the fast-moving consumer products market is that the market leader must increase its share of promotional support faster than the growth of promotional support of the total market otherwise there is a less than even chance of maintaining leadership.

Pepsi-Cola took the leadership away from the traditional leader, Coca-Cola, in the huge US foodstore market in 1977 where a single share point in the cola drinks market represented 23 million cases or nearly $140 million. Pepsico more than doubled its advertising expenditure between 1973 and 1977 while Coke's promotional expenditure remained static. To defend its leadership position in the foodstore market Pepsico continuously supported Pepsi-Cola at higher promotional levels than Coca-Cola's expenditure[7]. Following Miller Brewings' rapid increase in share of the US beer market, the leader, Anheuser-Busch, adopted a promotional support campaign in 1980 designed to solidify its precarious market share leadership over Miller. Anheuser-Busch increased its promotional support to $94 million, some $5 million greater than

Miller's expenditure, and together with a skilful segmentation campaign, obtained a volume growth twice that of Miller and almost three times that of the market, widening its leadership by taking almost 28% of the US beer market compared to Miller's 21% share.[8]

Resources

Company financial, productive, distributive, promotion, marketing and service resources can be combined to provide significant position defences against competitive challenges.

Almost on its own Caterpillar has managed to keep consistently ahead of its main competitors — Deere, JI Case, Clark Equipment, International Harvester and Komatsu of Japan — with a position defence strategy emphasizing resource utilization. Caterpillar has focused on three business areas — construction equipment, engines and materials handling — which are similar markets, utilizing the same dealer networks and thereby overcoming the need to concentrate expenditure on short-term requirements of numerous businesses. By focusing its resources almost single-mindedly on customer needs and how to meet these needs, Caterpillar has maintained its leadership of the market by building high quality, reliable products and ensuring complete servicing through extensive dealer networks[9].

IBM, which held as much as 60% of the US market for complex information processing in 1970, had fallen to a 32% share of the market in 1980 during which time the market grew nearly fivefold. In the mid-1970s as a resource position defence strategy IBM invested more than $4 billion in new plant and equipment world-wide to emphasize low-cost production. It also augmented its direct sales force for low priced products by selling small office products through independent distributors, mail order catalogues and company-owned retail stores, reorganized to position itself to attack the market-place segment by segment, and targeted its offensive against virtually every new growth area of the computer business from mainframe to personal computers. By mid 1984 IBM had increased its share to 75% of the mainframe computer market and 50% of the world's market for computers of all sizes.[10]

Line Extensions

The introduction of product and service extensions to the line are widely used position defence strategies where the defender uses the extension to broaden the product, to take the battle into new territory or into the challenger's territory, or to deflect and weaken the competitive thrust.

IBM, although the leading mainframe computer manufacturer, had continuously lost share to competitors marketing computers compatible with IBM's machines. The leading competitor, Amdahl, attracted buyers since its machines worked quickly, were cheap and could replace the IBM computers which some users found too small. In a position defence strategy IBM introduced a new range of computers in 1982 which reduced many of Amdahl's advantages. The new range of high performance computers could process instructions as well as the best of Amdahl's machines, and with improved air–cooling, matched Amdahl's speed and cost advantage. As the new IBM range could be rapidly upgraded in power this reduced the customers' need to purchase new machines. Amdahl was particularly vulnerable to the fall in demand for computers as much of its business came from customers that IBM was too busy to supply. With a slack demand, competitive machines and IBM's ability to deliver quickly Amdahl lost share to IBM.[11]

Federal Express, the leading US–based air courier, introduced its overnight express letter service as a line extension in 1981 to protect its leadership position in the overall air courier market. Following US Postal Service regulatory changes in 1979 which allowed for private delivery of 'extremely urgent' mail, Federal introduced its overnight letter service in 1981. By building up its position as the industry's lowest cost operator with heavy investment in aircraft and ground facilities and through its innovative 'hub–and–spoke' network of overnight air deliveries, Federal used its favourable cost position to introduce the new service at a penetration price to protect its main business. Competitors such as Airborne Express, Courier–Purolator and Emery Air Freight were faced with the dilemma of either entering the market with a difficult profit–generating position or of staying out of the market. By conceding the overnight letter business to Federal Express its competitors ran the risk of losing even more business as customers would be inclined to send everything through the same air courier.[12]

Chesebrough-Ponds has used a policy of continuous line extensions as part of its strategy to fight off attacks on its dominant share of the US spaghetti sauce market. In 1976, Extra Thick N' Zesty was introduced to foil Hunts' attack with Prima Salsa. Regular line extensions with Classic Combinations in 1978 and Pizza Quick Sauce in 1980 were again followed by Homestyle in 1981 to fend off Campbell Soups' attack with Prego. In contrast, the major national companies in the US breakfast market in the mid-1970s, Chock Full O'Nuts and Dunkin' Donuts, did not anticipate the possibility of McDonalds extending its opening hours to the early morning and competing with a full breakfast menu. McDonalds entered the early morning fast-food business in 1976 with its line extension breakfast menu including a new product, Egg McMuffin, and while taking business away from the major competitors, also expanded the overall breakfast market. McDonalds' line extension was so successful with consumers, and cost effective since the overheads were already partially covered by ongoing business, that by mid-1982 McDonalds was obtaining 40% of its US \$8 billion sales revenue from its line extension, breakfast market business.

Ownership

A common feature of current business combat is the acquisition of other companies as a means to obtain market position, growth, key business skills and resources. Since the prime goal of any company is to stay in business as an independent entity, position defence strategies have been used to fend off unwanted suitors who try to challenge the company's sovereignty by changing ownership through force.

A common defensive strategy is to fight takeover bids and proxy battles in public using the media to persuade shareholders to retain shares or hold out for a better offer. Predators frequently retaliate in kind. The battle by BTR to take over Thomas Tilling in the UK in 1983 cost between \$1.5 and \$3 million in newspaper space and Trafalgar House used an advertising agency, Saatchi & Saatchi, in its bid to sway shareholder opinion to take over P&O in 1983. Financial restructuring has also been used in position defence strategies. Lenox, a US china and glassware manufacturer, planned an innovative financial strategy to foil Brown-Forman's takeover bid. Lenox planned the distribution of a special dividend of 250,000 preferred shares which would have been convertible into common stock of any Lenox acquirer. This would have diluted the Brown family's 62% control of Brown-Forman. As a second phase of the defence Lenox planned the sale of convertible debentures to outside firms. Lenox' innovative strategy was not put into operation as Brown-Forman increased its offer to $90 per share which was finally accepted by the Lenox shareholders in 1983.

Also used is the 'White Knight' tactic where a company threatened by a hostile takeover bid finds a friendly partner which is a more acceptable suitor. However this can lead to extremely complex and costly battles where the suitors can outmanoeuvre themselves — a classic example being the Bendix, Martin Marietta, United Technologies triangle of 1982. Bendix a $4.4 billion conglomerate initially offered $43 per share, later raised to $48, for 55% of the equity of Martin a $3.3 billion aerospace company. Martin retaliated with a cash offer of $75 for 50.3% of the equity of Bendix. Martin also secured the help of a White Knight, United Technologies a $13.7 billion conglomerate, who would make a tender offer for Bendix if Martin's bid failed to succeed. Bendix increased its position to 70% of Martin's equity and Martin obtained 40% of the shares of Bendix. Bendix, fearing a hostile takeover by Martin backed by United Technologies brought out its own White Knight, Allied Chemical. A three way deal resulted where Allied merged with Bendix by buying both Martin's 46% of Bendix stock and the shares in public hands. As payment for Martin's block of Bendix shares, Allied relinquished Bendix' controlling interests in Martin. The hunter had become the prey.

Position defence strategies in war and business where a defender is faced with a determined aggressor invariably entail a siege situation which can prove costly. On the battlefield and in the market-place siege attacks are almost always successful against a position defence and there are strong precedents which suggest that a strategy which totally emphasizes fixed fortifications should be discounted as the initiative rests frequently with the attacker. It was said of Marshal Vauban, the greatest military engineer of the seventeenth century, who both built some 33 new fortresses and conducted 53 successful sieges that 'a town besieged by Vauban is a town taken'. Through the 18th century competence at siege warfare came to rival, and even surpass, battle skill as the chief professional requirement of a successful general. In business the parallel exists with executives who continually rely on position defences to stave off a competitive attack and who are rewarded for their defensive abilities rather than their competence in overall combat skills. As Peter Rumyantsen observed 'the objective is not the occupation of a geographic position but the destruction of enemy forces'.

MOBILE DEFENCE

'The Boers are not like the Sudanese who stood up to a fair fight. They are always running away on their little ponies'.

Lord Kitchener

Mobile defences are strategies designed to provide a defender with a flexible response to attack and hence the initiative.

In military combat both tactics and weaponry have been used to provide mobile defence; however, a true mobile defence depends largely on the mobility and manœuvrability of an armed force. Around 1200—1000 BC the horse was first used as a cavalry charger and remained the main form of armed mobility until the 1860s. It was at this time that von Moltke first used the railway for rapid mobilization and for transportation of supplies and reserves which proved so devastating in the Franco–Prussian War (1870—1871). The Boers (1899—1902) were highly successful in mobile defensive tactics using mounted marksmen with repeating rifles striking quickly before the unwieldy British forces, tied to the fixed railway system, could react. The US in Vietnam (1964—1975) used a combination of fortified position defences ('strategic hamlets') backed by tactical airpower and helicopter-borne 'air cavalry' as a mobile defence to counter-attacks by the highly mobile Viet Cong and North Vietnamese.

In business combat, mobile defensive moves are similar to those adopted by the military in that they attempt to blunt the enemy's offensive by shifting forces to meet an attack. Mobile defensive strategies in business focus around planned product replacement, product improvement and changes to the length and duration of the product life cycle. Conscious product development strategy provides the firm with the capability to be both proactive and reactive to competitive and environmental threats.

Gillette has maintained its 60% share of the $450 million US razor blade market by using a mobile defence strategy and has reduced its major competitors — American Safety Razor, Schick and Wilkinson's

Sword — to manufacturing similar versions of, and refill blades for, Gillette razors (see Figure 5.2). Gillette's strategy is to wait until its competitors get adjusted to one shaving system and then unleash yet another advance. For example the Techmatic system introduced in the late 1960s was successfully followed by the TRAC II system in 1971 and by the ATRA system in 1977. Each system formed the basis for a line of both up-market gift versions and special razors to tap the women's market such as the Daisy women's razor of 1974.[13]

Abbott Laboratories has successfully defended its US market share for the generic, or off-patent, antibiotic, erythromycin by introducing a series of replacement products, erythromycin stearate and ethinyl succinate, and a range of erythromycin dosage forms in special user packs to target on a wide range of needs from the pediatric market to full dose applications. The broad scale of mobile defence adopted by Abbott to support its highly priced branded product foiled the attack by much cheaper substitutes.

To protect its position as a leading manufacturer of pocket calculators Casio has adopted a highly successful mobile defence strategy, emphasizing rapid new product replacement designed to accelerate and shorten product life cycles. Casio has a functional strategy which integrates design and development into marketing so that Casio can respond suitably to changes in consumer needs. As Casio has this functional strategy well developed it can afford to obsolete its products quickly and put its competitors, who are vertically integrated and reliant on one to two year product life cycles, at a distinct disadvantage.[14]

In many firms the idea of planned product replacement appears to be an anathema since the replacement will cannibalize sales of an existing product. However, it is preferable to displace your own products, particularly if you can upgrade margins, than have a competitor do it for you.

The key to mobile defence strategy is to strike hard and fast at an attacker before he secures a viable position and, by blunting the offensive, secure the defence. The Argentines in a defensive position in the Falkland Islands (1982), did not take the initiative and foil the British sea-borne build-up with a mobile defensive strike before the Royal Navy had secured control of the sea-lanes and attained carrier-borne local air superiority. Similarly Boeing, Lockheed and McDonnell-Douglas did not take the initiative in the 220—345

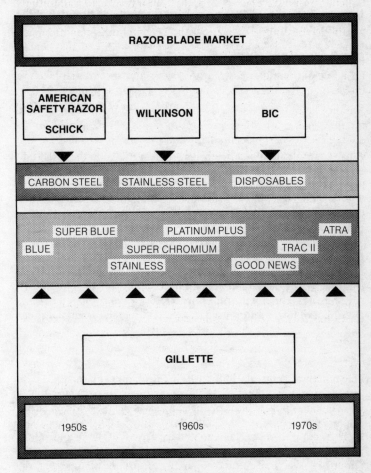

Figure 5.2
MOBILE DEFENCE

Gillette's 20 year mobile defence strategy to combat new competitive products in the world razor blade market.

seater short to medium range airliner market by developing their own products and were unable to meet the effective attack by Airbus Industrie with the A300B in a market formerly the preserve of the US aerospace industry.

PRE-EMPTIVE STRIKE

'Tora!, Tora!, Tora!'

> Japanese attack call-sign.
> Pearl Harbor (7 December 1941)

A pre-emptive strike is a defensive attack initiated in the belief that an enemy attack is imminent and that a first-strike will wreak such a physical and psychological blow that the enemy, caught unaware, will be either incapable of mounting a credible defence against future attacks for a period of time or will be forced to sue for terms.

Although Pearl Harbor (1941) epitomizes the pre-emptive strike this defensive strategy is as old as recorded history and has been practised continually through the centuries, the most recent example being the Israeli attack on Lebanon (1982).

In business combat the pre-emptive strike over competition takes a number of forms and is used as an attempt to maintain the status quo in favour of the defence (see Figure 5.3).

Resource Strikes

One of Dow Chemicals' hallmarks in the chemical industry is bold pre-emptive investment strikes for raw materials to ensure that it has a global supply of basic petrochemicals at the most advantageous prices.[15] Coca-Cola in the US in 1981 authorized its bottlers to use high-fructose corn sweetener to replace up to half the sugar in Coke to reap cost savings benefits as high-fructose generally sells for about 20% less than refined sugar. To ensure that its competitors could not immediately follow suit, Coca-Cola signed long-term purchase agreements tying-up most fructose capacity.[16]

Technology Strikes

The new biotechnologies developing in the late 1970s, offered the

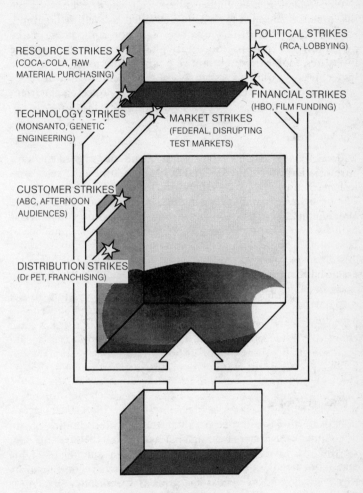

Figure 5.3
PRE-EMPTIVE STRIKES
Foiling potential competitive threats by conducting a strike before the competitive attack
develops.

opportunity for companies in a wide range of industries to achieve lower production costs, higher quality and new and more reliable raw material supplies for existing products as well as obtaining entirely new products. A number of major companies in the agriculture, chemicals, food, oil, pharmaceutical and mining industries, took early pre-emptive equity positions in the leading biotechnology companies such as Cetus, Genentech and Genex to acquire access to the technology as a means to protect their current and future markets.

Market Strikes

Federal Express conducted a successful pre-emptive stike against Airborne Express in the US in late 1980. Following the successful test marketing of Federal's new overnight express letter service, Airborne started similar test markets in Cleveland, Hartford and Philadelphia. Federal immediately entered Airborne's test markets with its own product which distorted the tests and siphoned off customers with Federal's better-known name.[17]

Financial Strikes

HBO, the leading cable TV network in the US, successfully uses a strategy of pre-production financing of films in return for exclusive pay TV viewing rights. These pre-emptive financing strikes have enabled HBO to obtain better deals with film companies, secure access to quality films, tighten its hold over the pay TV market and produce better profit margins than its cable TV competitors.

Customer Strikes

American Broadcasting Corporation (ABC) achieved an impressive pre-emptive customer strike against its CBS and NBC rivals with daytime TV serials in 1980. ABC produced a number of highly successful serial dramas aimed at women. On securing the majority of viewers, ABC developed a sales force to specifically sell daytime TV to advertisers. With a combination of high viewer ratings, lower advertising rates than evening prime-time TV, and lower production costs due to the use of lower paid actors and actresses and shooting on inexpensive sets, ABC achieved both a commanding position and a high return. ABC's six daytime serials earned an estimated

25% of ABC's sales revenues and 40% of its profits ($235 million) in 1983.[18]

Distribution Strikes

To pre-empt competition Doktor Pet, a pet franchising chain, signed leases in 150 shopping malls in the US whether the company had a franchisee lined-up or not. The foundation of prime leases ensured Doktor Pet's major position in the US pet franchising-market.[19]

In the early 1950s Timex revolutionized the market-place for watches in the US by introducing low-cost, almost disposable, mechanical watches marketed through a variety of retail outlets rather than through the traditional jewellery store distribution system. This distribution strike provided Timex with a lock on the low-cost watch market until displaced by electronic digital and quartz watches in the mid-1970s.

Political Strikes

Just when RCA's monochrome television system had reached the US market in 1947, CBS persuaded the FCC to make the jump to colour television using the CBS mechanical colour system. RCA, which had already invested heavily in its own colour system, was forced to initiate a rapid final development programme. RCA conducted a successful two-pronged political strike to head-off the CBS challenge. A formidable lobbying campaign was started by RCA in Washington to delay the FCC's decision on colour systems. RCA also lobbied for support from the US television manufacturers' National Television System Committee (NTSC) with an astute policy of freely turning over full design details of RCA's TV receiver to all manufacturers. Since RCA had its own major national TV broadcasting subsidiary (NBC) to initiate colour programmes, a TV manufacturing subsidiary, and since the RCA colour system was compatible with the existing (RCA) monochrome system, the FCC selected the NTSC (or RCA) system as the TV colour standard for the US.

Not all pre-emptive strikes are successful either in war or in business. When Mastercard announced in 1977 that it was launching a travellers cheque system, its arch rival VISA quickly up–staged Mastercard by launching its travellers cheques first. However, by late 1981, none of the 13 banks issuing VISA travellers cheques were making a profit. VISA underestimated the length of time that it would take for travellers cheques to become profitable and the emergence of two companies in the market in such a short time triggered a price war which benefitted no–one except the third-party agent banks selling their cheques.[20] While pre–emptive strikes provide the defender with the initiative they are short–term solutions to business conflict. Unless the potential aggressor is forced completely from the market–place there is a continuous challenge to the defender.

FLANK POSITIONING

'We must therefore turn towards the flanks of the enemy's position'.

Feldmarschall Helmuth, Graf von Moltke

A flank positioning defensive strategy is designed to place part of the defensive force in a position to outflank offensive manœuvres by an aggressor.

The defensive battle at Buena Vista in the Mexican–American War (1846—1847) fought by the Americans against Santa Anna, was successful since Jefferson Davies defeated the Mexican attempt to turn Zachary Taylor's flank. This placed the Americans in a position to outflank the Mexicans and precipitated the collapse of Santa Anna's offensive which virtually ended the war in North Mexico.

In business combat, the direct parallel with flank positioning is the repositioning of a product or service in the market–place or the repositioning of resources to meet expected competitive thrusts.

Market Repositioning

When the US tyre market slowed down in the early 1980s Armstrong Rubber, the sixth largest US tyre manufacturer, conducted a flank positioning defensive strategy to maintain its 9% market share, and the 70% of Armstrong's corporate sales derived from the tyre market (see Figure 5.4). Armstrong repositioned to its strong niche in the replacement tyre market which it serviced through 1,000 independent distributors, and through Sears Roebuck which purchased up to 40% of Armstrong's tyres for resale through its in–store auto-

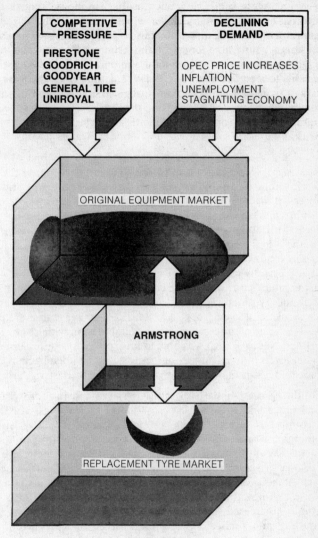

Figure 5.4
FLANK POSITIONING
Armstrong Rubber's flank positioning response to competitive threats and changing market
conditions in the US tyre market.

servicing outlets. Increasing new car prices in the US forced many
motorists to keep their cars longer, which broadened the market for
replacement tyres. Unlike the larger companies — Goodyear,
Firestone, Uniroyal, Goodrich and General Tire — who were
heavily dependent on the original equipment market, Armstrong
was able to increase unit sales by 11% at a time when the total unit
market increased by 2%. Armstrong's flank positioning move
anticipated the market change and the firm reacted well before the
larger companies could mount an effective attack on Armstrong's-
position.[21]

New York Air, founded in 1981, was one of the first airlines,
following de-regulation of the US airline industry, to use the low
fare formula to enter the market. New York Air was initially
successful in entering the north-east corridor market and obtained
a viable market share. When the major airlines, led by Eastern,
successfully fought back with predatory pricing, New York Air
became a loss-maker, remaining solvent only through a series of
cash injections from its parent, Texas Air Corporation. New York
Air successfully repositioned itself in the market early in 1983 as a
businessman's airline. By increasing comfort with a 34-inch seat
pitch and by providing frills, including free weekday newspapers,
free drinks and 'New York style' snacks, together with a 'frequent
flyers' scheme of mileage awards in collaboration with Continental
Airlines, New York Air was able to raise prices to similar and even
higher levels than its major competitors and climbed back into the
black and again mounted a serious challenge to Eastern Airlines.

Scandinavian Airlines (SAS), although a year late in comparison to
Air France and British Airways, adopted the business class and
discount fare layout in its aircraft in late 1981. By using a
combination of tactics SAS carried out a successful flank positioning
defence. While the other carriers had introduced their business
classes with a surcharge over full economy fares, SAS introduced its
'First' Business Class at economy class fares without a surcharge.
While cutting administrative overheads by some 20—25%, SAS
actually increased investment in check-in counters, baggage
handling and service training for staff at all levels within the
company. With this market repositioning strategy emphasizing
service, SAS flew slightly fewer passengers in 1982 over 1981 but
managed to transfer 6% of the reduced fare passengers into its 'First'

Business Class with fares about double those of the discount fares. The effects on revenues, profits and market shares for SAS, both in Scandinavia and internationally, were dramatic.[22]

Failure to note the warning signs of the need to reposition products in the market can lead to almost fatal situations.

Izod, the Alligator brand shirtmaker which had a phenomenal growth in the US where sales doubled between 1979 and 1982, began to decline as a result of the failure to reposition its product. In the late 1970s the Alligator brand shirt became a hot fashion item and Izod could not produce enough shirts to meet demand. This enabled a number of 'animal' clones — fox, tiger and horse brands — to enter the market to meet the demand. Izod failed to capitalize on the Alligator shirts' popularity and update its primary colour sportswear line. When fashion moved away from primary colours to pastel colours, stripes and variations of the basic shirt, Izod clung to its old line. The clones moved quickly to meet the change and began to market a total look of shirts, trousers, sweaters and accessories offering complete lines and the chance for multiple sales for retailers. This had the effect of pushing Izod out of prime selling space in retail outlets further depressing Izod's sales.

Resource Repositioning

Racal Electronics, acquired Decca in the UK in 1980 as a flank positioning defensive strategy. Decca possessed a number of product lines such as microwave–frequency radios and electronic warfare systems which Racal needed to fill gaping holes in its coverage of the military communications market. Since the majority of customers for Racal were governments who preferred that one supplier assume total responsibility for their military's entire electronic needs, the acquisition of Decca enabled Racal to reposition its resources to increase Racal's overall share of individual contracts and reduce the inefficient method of building consortiums of companies with complementary products to meet military contracts. In addition, Decca's technological expertise in radar and computers offered Racal the opportunity to diversify away from its heavy reliance on military radios and data transmission gear into new growth areas.[23]

Blue Bell, the second largest jeans and apparel manufacturer in the USA acquired Jantzen, a producer of swimwear, sweaters, shirts, blouses and dresses in 1980. Blue Bell's acquisition of Jantzen's resources was a classic flank positioning defence. Jantzen, located on the West coast, offered the opportunity, through existing warehouses, for Blue Bell to step up distribution of its existing products (notably Wrangler Jeans), in the West where it was weak in comparison to its arch rival Levi Strauss. In addition, Blue Bell's strength was in bargain basements and discount stores. Jantzen also offered Blue Bell the opportunity to move into the mid-priced high margin apparel market favoured by specialty and department stores.[24]

The success of flank positioning defence depends on the ability of the defender to anticipate future aggressive moves and the relative strength of the flank position. An excellent example of both factors in a military context was the reliance of the Japanese in the Pacific (1941—1945) on the fortified island concept. From a fixed series of positions, the Japanese gave the initiative to the US and did not anticipate future US offensive moves in the Pacific. The Allied bypass strategy effectively isolated many of the fortified islands and reduced the ability of the Japanese to conduct flank positioning moves against the Allies.

Both factors appear in business combat. Pepsi-Cola anticipated that Seven-Up's aggressive 1982 promotion of its caffeine-free cola product, Like, could make major inroads into Pepsi's leading position in the US soft drinks market, dominated by cola products which contained caffeine. Pepsi-Cola quickly formulated a 99% caffeine-free cola, Pepsi-Free and backed by $100 million advertising campaign aggressively promoted the product as a flank positioning strategy to protect its overall position in the soft drinks market from the threat of Seven-Up's Like.[25]

A flank positioning defence suffers from the same drawbacks as a flanking attack, that is, the weakening of the centre to protect the flank. Much of early military strategy was based on envelopment where both combatants took steps to meet and counter the others' moves by placing a blocking force in the path of each flanking movement. Eventually this led to the stalemate conditions of continuous fronts experienced in the First World War.

The analogy in business combat is the continuous expansion of the product line with new models introduced to fill product line gaps more thoroughly by offering options or accessories, which literally individualize products, to cover the sub-markets in greater depth. This allows trade-up on the company's product line through planned overlap. While this strategy was successful for the US car industry in the 1950s and 1960s, it proved disastrous against the Japanese assault in the 1970s. The Japanese offered a small range of fully-equipped cars at low prices, a strategy which punched a hole through the US car industry's individualized product approach, where dealer profits were heavily weighted to the number of options ordered by customers.

COUNTER-OFFENCE

'To every blow struck in war there is a counter'.

Sir Winston Churchill (1939)

The counter-offensive is the classical response to an attack where the objective is to wrest the initiative from the attacker by foiling the attack through a counter-stroke.

Although Robert Clive's force of 3,000 was greatly outnumbered by Siraj-Ud-Daula's 52,000 men at the Battle of Plessey (1757), Clive counter-attacked so successfully from his position defence that the Indians recoiled and withdrew, and left the British East India Company virtually in control of the vast province of Bengal. In more modern times the Japanese counter-offensives at Kohima and Imphal (1944) were primarily directed at safeguarding the vulnerable Japanese position in Burma by spoiling the Allied offensive that was clearly being prepared in India.

There are strong analogies between military and business counter-offences.

Product Counter-offensive

The Swiss watch industry suffered major sales declines as a result of overlooking the importance of electronic and digital watches, underestimating the aggressive marketing of Casio, Citizen and Seiko, and failing to counter the phenomenal rise in the exchange rate of the Swiss franc. By early 1983 the Swiss watch industry was in serious trouble. The leading companies ASUAG (watch parts) and SSIH (the Certina, Longines, Rado and Tissot brands) saw their world market shares fall from 30% in the early 1970s to 9%. They had lost the volume sector of the market to low cost watches from Hong Kong and Taiwan and were being threatened by Citizen and Seiko who were moving into the higher quality high margin products which made up the backbone of ASUAG–SSIH's business. In 1983, following government and bank loans of 950 million Swiss francs, ASUAG and SSIH merged into IHSSA and began a belated counter–attack. The counter–attack was based on a new product — the Swatch — a low cost electronic quartz fashion watch. Using industrial robots to cut production costs, and advanced technology in the form of a hardened resin case which was virtually indestructible and unaffected by shock or temperature changes, the Swatch was packed in a case 8mm thick and weighing 20 grams, and in a variety of colours to match fashions. Supported by heavy promotion and sold through jewellery stores the Swatch, retailing at a cost of $20, was designed to both capitalize on the image of Swiss quality and generate sufficient revenue to bring IHSSA into a profit within three years.

In early 1979 McDonalds, the world's largest restaurant chain, was faced with stagnating sales as a result of soaring costs of food and increasing costs of fuel which forced more families to eat at home. In addition, competition from exotic fast–food chains, especially pizza houses, fish and chip shops and taco bars, began to attract customers away from McDonalds prime product, the hamburger. To spice up its business, McDonalds counter–attacked by introducing a chopped steak sandwich in 1979, its first new product since 1972. This was followed by a fish fillet, McFish, and in 1981, a national (US) launch of a poultry sandwich, Chicken McNuggets, in an attempt to provide the evening variety needed to attract families. By 1983 Chicken McNuggets accounted for 12% of McDonalds' $8.2 billion sales, of which 60% was purely incremental growth.[26]

IBM had dominated the world electro–mechanical typewriter market for over 15 years with its limited line of Selectric and Executive typewriters. Complacency brought on neglect and IBM was faced with a serious threat to its business on the introduction of new and superior electronic typewriters, notably the QYX Intelligent Typewriter. IBM belatedly began a product counter–offensive and started the phase–out of the Selectric and Executive models in late 1978 and replaced them with a new line of electronic typewriters offering a range of new features to combat QYX.

The 'fighting brand' concept is widely used as a counter-attack strategy. Folgers coffee gained market share rapidly at the expense of the US market leader, General Foods' Maxwell House brand. General Foods counter-attacked by launching a new brand, Horizon, which had similar taste characteristics and packaging design to Folgers to deflect the attack on Maxwell House.

When San Miguels' 92 year monopoly of the Philippine beer market was challenged in 1982 by Asia Brewery's pilsner, Beer Hausen, San Miguel introduced its own pilsner, Gold Eagle, backed by a heavy promotional campaign to deflect Beer Hausan's thrust.[27] Seiko facing strong pressure from Casio and a number of manufacturers from Taiwan and Hong Kong in the low priced electronic quartz watch market introduced its own low priced Alba, Lorus and Pulsar brands through mass merchandizers as fighting brands to protect the low priced end of its business which accounted for 60% of Seiko's sales.

Promotional Counter-offensive

R.J. Reynolds, the market leader in the US cigarette market, saw its market share stagnate in the 1970s at around 32% while Philip Morris' increased from 18% to 31%. Reynolds counter-attacked with both revamped marketing strategies and new products to deflect Philip Morris' attack on its leadership position. Reynolds realigned its advertising practices from its previous reliance on cost-efficiency which created heavy dependence on mass-circulation magazines which produced 'clutter' with a number of brands in the same magazine as well as placing cigarettes smoked mainly by men into women's magazines. In 1980 Reynolds moved promotion to carefully targeted audiences and into newspapers and outdoor signs. In addition, line extensions were created in the same style as that of the original brand to yield a 'family' umbrella under which the brands could be advertised without splitting product image. New products, Salem and Vantage Ultra Lights, were introduced to tap the explosive growth in low tar brands (those with 15mg of tar or less) which grew from a 2% share of the total market in 1974 to 40% in 1980.[28]

Apple Computer came under heavy attack from IBM and Tandy in late 1981 in the US personal computer market. Apple, with neither the massive direct sales force of IBM or the large chain of Radio Shack retail stores operated by Tandy, depended on an independent dealer network to market its products. Apple counter-attacked with a television advertising campaign to generate a high level of consumer awareness to push customers into its dealer network, to offset IBM's marketing and Tandy's distribution strengths.[29]

Production Counter-offensive

Following the successful attack by Michelin on the US tyre market with its combination of radial tyre technology and low cost non-unionized plants in the Southern states, which was heightened by the OPEC price increases, the US tyre manufacturers counter-attacked. Between 1975 and 1980, nearly 20 plants were closed, most of them with bias or cross-ply tyre production lines. Despite considerable losses, the US tyre manufacturers spent heavily on converting to radial tyre production in new, cost-efficient plants, in the largely non-union Southern States to provide a low cost challenge to Michelin.[30]

Jaguar, despite the tag of being an expensive and luxurious sporting car manufacturer, had a bad reputation for supply, quality and reliability. By late 1979, Jaguar was losing money and had the lowest output of vehicles in its recent history. Following the split-off of Jaguar as a separate company from British Leyland in 1980, a major production counter-offensive involving engineered reliability, quality construction and supplier responsibility was instituted. By 1982, the company had increased the quality and reliability of Jaguar cars to such an extent that a re-launch of the marque in Europe was scheduled for later in that year. A major investment programme was initiated to replace the XJ6 saloon and the existing engine, as the company reached break-even point and was profitable again at the end of 1982. By 1983 Jaguar sales had reached £450 million with profits of more than £30 million.[31]

Financial Counter-offensive

Lorimar, an independent film production company whose films included the phenomenally successful 'Dallas' television series, acquired a New York advertising agency, Kenyon & Eckhardt, for $21 million in 1983 as a financial counter-offensive. Lorimar and other independent film production companies were squeezed by high production costs and fickle audience ratings, and were too small to get either higher prices from the major networks or cable services, or a share of the advertising revenue generated by their films. Lorimar's financial counter-offensive was designed to secure production funding from large advertisers, using the Kenyon & Eckhardt agency, so that the film, complete with advertisements, could be sold in a package deal direct to the cable networks. By securing pre-production film financing and a tie-in with major advertisers, Lorimar counted on increasing its bargaining power with the cable networks to increase its margins.

Alliance Counter-offensive

Philips introduced the first commercial videotape recorder in 1972 — well ahead of Sony and Matsushita. Early technical snags, poor marketing and a lack of pre-recorded tapes for users left Philips vulnerable to the Japanese invasion in the late 1970s. The wide range of video recorders priced to suit customer's budgets, an array of pre-recorded tapes together with an aggressive licensing policy by Matsushita, eroded Philips' market share in the early years. In 1982, Philips started a counter-offensive with its new VC 2000 system. The new system was superior to current Japanese technology offering high quality replay and a range of sophisticated features. A highly automated plant, a marketing alliance linking up with Grundig to provide a strong European distribution network and the fortuitous sharp climb of the yen against European currencies provided Philips with an opportunity to breach the Japanese dominated video-recorder market.[32]

Combination Counter-offensive

Atari, holding 75% of the US video-game market, unleashed a major combination counter-offensive in 1982 in an attempt to maintain its leading position. Atari's counter-attack was based on a network TV campaign ($15 million) supported by dealer co-operative advertisements ($15 million) and radio spots backed by magazine advertisements. Atari also doubled the pace of introduction of new game cartridges to both fend off competitors marketing Atari-compatible game cartridges and to increase existing customer loyalty. In addition, they developed a co-sponsored contest costing $20 million for Atari products with the McDonalds fast food chain to reinforce its position amongst children and youths.[33]

American Express, the world-wide leader in travel and entertainment credit cards, was faced in late 1981 with a massive assault from both its traditional competitors Carte Blanche and Diners Club, and from new offerings from Mastercard and Visa supported by groups of international banks. American Express responded with a combination counter-offence by virtually removing the minimum income requirement for its traditional Green Card and introducing a Gold Card providing extra services such as a loan facility. Also American Express' merger with Shearson Loeb Rhohdes, the Wall Street securities firm, provided a base for offering innovative investment services not available to the US commercial banks.[34]

Kodak, faced with a major challenge to its leading position in the US film market from Fuji in the late 1970s, used a combination counter-offensive to overcome the thrust against its core business. Kodak cut prices and launched a major advertising campaign to encourage customers to ask for Kodak paper by name. This was assisted by increasing support services for photofinishers including a sophisticated computer-aided fault diagnosis service. By 1981, Kodak's share had increased to around 65% of the market from its low of 50% in 1977, mainly at the expense of Fuji.[35]

Chesebrough-Ponds' success with Vaseline Intensive Care Lotion in the US hand-care lotion market attracted Procter & Gamble. In 1977 P&G moved into the market with Wondra Skin Conditioning Lotion. Chesebrough retaliated with a combination counter-attack which consisted of a new product launch of Ponds Cream and Cocoa Butter Lotion to confuse P&G's attack and disrupting Wondra's test markets with a 10 ounce, two-for-the-price-of-one offer for Vaseline Intensive Care Lotion. This stalled P&G long enough for Chesebrough to develop and push its 'enriched' Vaseline Intensive Care Lotion directly against Wondra. By the end of 1980 Chesebrough still held more than 25% of the market while P&G at third place held a bare 8% of the US hand-care lotion market.

In the 1970s Scott Paper, a major US supplier of paper towels and toilet tissue faced strong competitive attacks from Procter & Gamble, Georgia Pacific and Ft. Howard Paper who successfully took major pieces of the business away from Scott Paper. Scott

Paper developed a combination counter-offensive strategy to protect its business (see Figure 5.5). A strategy was adopted of pouring money into products that had a chance to be leaders and reducing expenditure on the rest. Some well-known brands including, Cottonette and Soft'n'Pretty tissues introduced in the 1970s to combat Procter & Gamble's market leader Charmin, were de-emphasized. A combination of 'milking', repositioning and withdrawal strategies were adopted for Scotkins and Western Living napkins, Confidents sanitary napkins, Soft-Weve tissue and a line of specialty and converting papers. Scott Paper also invested $2 billion over five years to make the company the lowest cost producer of toilet paper (Scottissue, Family Scott, Waldorf), paper towels (Scottowels, Viva, Job Squad), facial tissues (Scotties), certain napkins and a baby wipe. Scott Paper also increased its emphasis internationally by moving into Korea and Malaysia and expanded existing plants in Mexico, Taiwan and the Philippines.[36]

By 1980 Vauxhall's position in the UK car market had deteriorated to an 8% market share and with a demoralized dealer network, a fractious workforce, and a reputation for rust, its survival was in doubt. A combination counter-offensive was evolved to deal with each of these core problems. The dealer network was pruned and strengthened by incorporating dealerships for Opel in 1981 which increased the number of cars sold by dealers by over 115% in two years. Vauxhall's two UK plants were re-organized and the workforce cut to increase quality and productivity. The Cavalier General Motors' $5 billion 'world car', was introduced in 1981 and by early 1984 had become the second bestselling car in the UK. Quality improvements, which slashed warranty costs, and the Cavalier's success, created interest in Vauxhall's small Astra and Nova cars, and in the larger Carlton(Senator) car. Vauxhall's successful counter-offensive increased sales by 44% to a record 262,000 cars in 1983, bringing Vauxhall close to break-even point. By early 1984 Vauxhall's share of new car sales reached 18.7% of the market, behind Ford's 28.1% share, but pushing BL(at 17.8%) into third place for the first time.

While counter-offensives may result in tactical successes, they can lead to strategic failures. The three Ludendorf counter-offensives in March to May 1918 were brilliant tactical successes pushing the British far beyond the Somme and the French back to the Meuse.

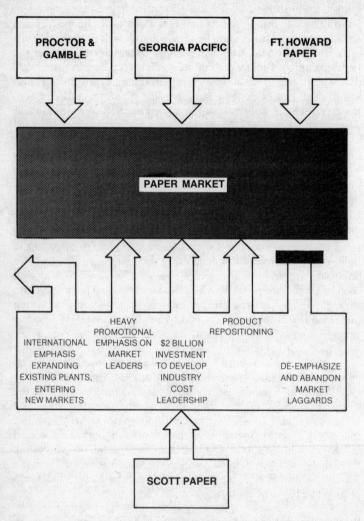

Figure 5.5
COMBINATION COUNTER-OFFENCE
Scott Paper's combination counter-offence to combat the attacks by FT. Howard Paper, Georgia Pacific and Proctor & Gamble on its share in the US paper products market.

However, the fourth of the offensives on the Marne was fully anticipated and met by a devastating French–US counter–offensive at Château–Thierry and South of the Aisne. In early August, the British broke through the German lines at the Somme and the German retreat did not stop until the Armistice in 1918. While Freddy Laker's Skytrain proved to be a devastating blow to the scheduled airlines and a tactical success, it ended as a strategic failure when the scheduled airlines responded with the same discounted fares, syphoning–off much of the new market which Laker Airways had created.

An acute sense of timing is critical for a successful counter–offensive as are the resources necessary to sustain the offence. While the German counter–offensive in the Ardennes (1944) was brilliantly timed and executed, the Wehrmacht did not have the resources to sustain the offence and was forced to retreat after its initial success. While Laker Airways counter–attacked against the matching discounted fares of the scheduled airlines with various classes of fares and special services, the airline did not have the resources to fight a long war of attrition.

STRATEGIC WITHDRAWAL

'We are not retreating. We are merely attacking in another direction'.
Major–General Oliver Smith, Chosin Reservoir, Korea
(November 1950)

Almost all armies and companies at one time or another, however competently led, armed and supplied, have been forced to conduct strategic withdrawals. The object of a strategic withdrawal, a defensive manœuvre, is to extricate the maximum amount of men and material from an untenable position and to provide an opportunity to regroup, re–arm and replenish. The North African deserts of Egypt and Libya provided excellent tank terrain for offensive thrusts. With little terrain advantage for either the opposing British or Italo–German forces, the Desert campaign of 1940—1942 was characterized by a number of strategic withdrawals by both sides as the advantage of quality of arms and supplies ebbed and flowed between the combatants. In the Arab–Israeli War of October 1973 the Egyptians achieved total surprise, and broke through the Israeli fortified east bank of the Suez Canal in overwhelming force. The Israelis made a rapid strategic withdrawal to regroup, re-arm and replenish before conducting a successful counter-offensive.

While standing and holding a position against all odds has a long military history and projects a courageous image, unless that action is part of an overall defensive strategy it is nothing more than a futile gesture. The French at Dien Bien Phu (1954) were isolated in an indefensible position and supplied by air which was vulnerable to ground fire. The Viet Minh were eventually successful in denying air resupply and casualty evacuation, and in holding up relief columns, and Dien Bien Phu fell after six months and a siege of 54 days.

In similar vein to military combat, companies have frequently been forced to make strategic withdrawals in the face of untenable product, social, political or technological conditions.

Product Failure

— Where a company can no longer compete effectively with its products or services in terms of cost, price, delivery, quality and credit against its opponents' product and service offerings.

Du Pont introduced Corfam, a synthetic leather substitute in 1964. Shoes made with Corfam lasted virtually forever and were not considered much of a boom in the fashion-conscious free-spending market of the 1960s when shoe leather was relatively inexpensive and other leather substitutes such as vinyl were even cheaper. As a result of a timing failure, a misunderstanding of the market-place and of competition, Corfam was withdrawn in 1971 and Du Pont took a tax write-off of $100 million.[37]

In 1981, Johnson & Johnson withdrew from the US disposable diaper market with an estimated charge against earnings of $14—16 million. J&J's fate was sealed when Procter & Gamble, which already led the market with Pampers, introduced its Luvs brand in 1978. Luvs, a contoured diaper with elasticated leg bands was followed by Kimberly-Clark's Huggies which also had elasticated leg bands, both of which were considered by consumers to be superior to the J&J brand. J&J did not follow suit and match competitive product quality or meet consumer desires and lost share to below 10% of the market in late 1980 at which point costs were no longer covered.[38]

Lockheed began work on the L1011 Tristar aircraft in 1968 and delivered the first aircraft to Eastern Airlines in 1972. The Tristar was a late third into the large, wide-bodied jet airliner market after Boeing and McDonnell-Douglas and was unable to attract sufficient orders. By late 1981 the company had sustained a loss of $2.5 billion on the Tristar programme and Lockheed was forced to phase the L1011 out of production. Lockheed left the commercial aviation market in early 1982.[39]

Procter & Gamble developed and marketed Pringle, a potato-snack product, in 1968. Using expertise in oil technology, P&G offered Pringle in a convenient canister pack and guaranteed unbroken, uniform-size chips. Pringle went national in 1975 with a $75 million promotional campaign and achieved 25% of the fragmented market largely made up of regional brands. Sales began to falter as customers, after the novelty of the package and product wore off, objected to the taste. Despite new flavours, sales began to drop and by 1980 Pringle's market share had fallen to 3% of the potato-snack market which forced P&G to cut advertising and research and close one of the brand's two production plants.[40]

Both Gillette in the US, and Sinclair in Europe, abandoned their assaults on the digital watch market in the late 1970s. Aggressive pricing, cost leadership strategies and rapid new product development by existing competitors created unattractive margins for Gillette and strained the financial resources of Sinclair.

Social Withdrawal

— When a company is forced by social pressures to withdraw from the market-place.

Ralph Nader conducted a successful public campaign in the 1960s against General Motors' Chevrolet Corvair on safety grounds which forced General Motors to eventually withdraw the car from the market.

Johnson & Johnson temporarily withdrew its Tylenol analgesic in the US in 1982 as a result of deaths caused by a third party adulterating the product with cyanide. Tylenol with $400 million in sales held one-third of the US analgesic market and accounted for some 15% of Johnson & Johnsons' $468 million net earnings in 1981. The recall costs after taxes were estimated at $50 million in 1982.

Procter & Gamble withdrew its Rely tampon from the US market in September 1980 after US Government researchers reported that in one study, over 70% of patients with toxic-shock syndrome, a sometimes fatal disease, had worn the Rely brand. Proctor & Gamble took a $75 million write-off on its Rely business in 1981.[41]

Technological Withdrawal

— When a company is forced to retreat from the market due to the superiority of competitive technology and the lack of internal-technological resources.

During the 1970s, the AM radio stations in the US were gradually forced out of the mainstream of radio broadcasting as the low quality signal made it impossible for AM stations to match the stereo quality sound of FM radio stations. By the late 1970s the FM stations had moved from the beautiful music format through progressive rock to the pop chart, forcing AM stations to withdraw into the less lucrative low audience markets for news, sports and talk shows.[42]

EMI pioneered the co-axial tomography (CAT) scanner in the early 1970s, which earned EMI £38 million profits on sales of £161 million between 1974 and 1977. Increased Government regulations on health care expenditure in the largest market, the US, led to a slump in sales which was exacerbated by a successful counter-attack from the traditional manufacturers of X-Ray machines with their own second generation CAT scanners and compounded by EMI's own production difficulties. The drain on resources, particularly for heavy development expenses on EMI's second generation CAT scanner, CT 7070, was partially the cause of EMI's purchase by Thorn Electric in 1979. Thorn, with a balance sheet badly weakened by the EMI purchase, sold out the CAT scanner business to General Electric of the US in 1980, which gave General Electric, already a CAT scanner producer, a commanding position in the market.[43]

Exxon purchased Reliance Electric in 1979 for $1.2 billion, to obtain

Reliance's potential energy saving device, an alternating–current synthesizer. In the Spring of 1981, Exxon announced the abandoning of the product due to research problems. Although the loss was estimated at $15 million, the amount of R&D that Exxon had invested, it was believed that the write–off was in the region of $600 million representing the premium that Exxon paid for Reliance in the belief that the synthesizer was ready to bring to market.[44]

Political withdrawal

— Where a company is forced to withdraw from a market as a direct or indirect result of political pressures.

BOAC was forced by direct UK Government pressure to abandon its profitable West African routes in 1971 in favour of British Caledonian Airlines to meet the Conservative Government's policy to support a private enterprise second airline on international routes.

Coca–Cola and IBM withdrew from India in 1978 as a result of indirect pressures by the Indian Government who required technology and process information transfer to Indian companies and the Foreign Exchange Regulations Act (1973) which excluded expatriate companies from holding more than 40% of the equity of their Indian subsidiaries.

Playboy Enterprises withdrew from its $135 million Atlantic City Hotel/Casino operation when the company was unable to secure a New Jersey gambling licence in mid–1982. The inability of Playboy to secure a New Jersey licence was based on the loss of the company's gaming licences in the UK for alleged credit violations.[45]

Both armies and firms have a knack of not knowing when to make a strategic withdrawal from the battlefield or market by gauging that point at which further conflict will have serious implications for the continued existence of an army or firm as an independent entity. A combination of ego, tunnel vision, misplaced optimism, vested interests and plain lack of knowledge frequently deflect generals and executives from making the right decision to withdraw.

Braniff International Airlines went bankrupt in 1982 as a result of adopting a number of disastrous defensive strategies which had the cumulative effect of forcing the airline out of business. In 1978,

Braniff joined the competitive fight to open up new routes following de-regulation. In the months following de-regulation, Braniff introduced a myriad of routes to 16 new cities in the US and four destinations each in Europe and the Far East. Although new aircraft were purchased for these routes, Braniff's costs in opening these routes, together with new aircraft finance charges and high operating costs of both old DC-8s on Latin American routes and fuel hungry short-bodied 727 aircraft on shorter routes placed severe strains on the airline's finances. The decline in airline travel due to the recession and heavy discounting of tickets to stave off challenges by American and Southwest Airlines finally exhausted Braniff's credit line and forced the airline out of business.

In contrast, Boussois-Souchon-Neuvesel (BSN), the second largest French glass producer, deriving 95% of its revenues from flat glass sales in the late 1960s, conducted a successful policy of strategic withdrawl from the glass industry emphasizing growth in other areas. BSN recognized that to maintain its share in the glass market involved continuous and heavy capital investment and that strong competition brought low returns on its investments. Since BSN was a large-scale glass bottle producer, it elected to start its diversification by buying large market share businesses with liquids to fill its bottling capacity. Purchases of Kronenburg and Société Européene de Brassèries gave BSN 45% of the French beer market and BSN, through its acquisition of Evian, obtained one third of the French market for mineral water. Further diversification in 1973, which brought in the dairy products firm Gervais-Danone, pushed the food and drinks share of BSN's business to more than 50% of its resources. With its new business portfolio established, BSN returned to its glass business and for six years stopped its acquisition programme and reinvested 3 billion french francs in modernizing its glass production facilities. By 1980 BSN's glass plants were in good enough shape to sell its West German Flachglas operations to Pilkington, its Belgian (Glaverbel) and Dutch (de Maas) operations to Asahi and its French plants to PPG Industries. BSN then used the proceeds from the sale of its glass operations to finance the international expansion of its food and drink portfolio. BSN's strategic withdrawl transformed the company within a decade from France's second largest glass manufacturer to its largest food group, and from stagnant sales and low profits to revenues of FF21.4 billion and profits of FF574 million in 1983.[46]

The quotation from Musarum Delicate in the seventeenth century; 'He that fights and runs away may live to fight another day', is as true for military combat as it is for business combat and has lost none of its meaningfulness over the centuries. Fighting for lost causes is a sure way to destruction. Under any conditions companies need the flexibility to divest themselves rapidly of businesses where opportunity turns to threat as competitive and environmental change alter the state of the market.

SUMMARY

While defence is essential to protect a battlefield or a market position, both armies and firms have still to learn that no defence with any strategy is impregnable and given sufficient time and effort to develop new weapons and tactics and to build up resources all defences can be overwhelmed.

Defensive measures have long been used as a means of signalling a potential aggressor that attack will be met by counterforce. Throughout history, however, a problem has existed with defensive measures used to discourage aggression since belligerents do not always share the beliefs and practices central to the defenders idea of the status quo, nor is an aggressor necessarily deterred by the amount or quality of the defence. The Wehrmacht was not deterred by the Maginot line in France in 1940 nor was Israel deterred in 1967 from conducting a simultaneous blitzkrieg attack on Egypt, Jordan and Syria which possessed collectively larger and better armed forces in excellent defensive positions. Similarly, IBM was not deterred from entering the personal computer market in 1981 despite the five year market advantage of its rivals, the highly competitive nature of the market (with 150 companies), consumer marketing techniques new to IBM, and the domination of the market by the personal computer innovator, Apple.

The two key issues in defensive combat revolve around the strength of the defence and the value of the position. The first imperative is whether the defences are strong enough to withstand a major attack without weakening the entire army or company. General Henri Navarre clearly underestimated the strength of the Viet Minh and overestimated the strength of the French position at

Dien Bien Phu (1954). The subsequent defeat of the French broke their resolve to continue the war and the French withdrew from Indo-China. Lockheed underestimated the early competitive lead and marketing strength of Boeing and McDonnell-Douglas and was forced to abandon the L1011 Tristar in 1982 as the drain on corporate resources was dragging Lockheed towards insolvency.

The second imperative is whether the position is worth defending at all costs. Generals and executives have a marked inclination to defend positions beyond their realistic strategic value — with inevitable results. The battle for Guadalcanal (1942—1943) involved an island that neither the Japanese or the US really wanted but which neither side could afford to abandon to the other. The battle resulted in large human and material losses for both sides. In 1976, Gillette was forced to introduce its Good News disposable shaver as a defensive measure to counter the disposable BIC shaver. While Gillette succeeded in overhauling BIC in the disposable razor market, Gillette won a pyrrhic victory. As Gillette already held a commanding 60% of the US razor blade market and the key to success in the disposable segment was price, on a per blade basis Gillette generated lower revenues with its Good News than on its conventional high cost lines since Gillette had to supply the handle as well as the cartridge. Every time Good News gained a share point of the overall razor blade market, Gillette lost millions of dollars.[47] Schering-Plough in a bid to retain a large part of the business when its leading antibiotic drug, Garamycin, went off patent in 1980, slashed unit prices by as much as 70% in 12 months. While Schering won the battle and managed to keep three quarters of the unit volume, it lost the war as sales revenue in 1981 fell below $30 million compared to $90 million in 1980 and Garamycin's contribution to profits fell from 35% to under 10% as a result of its drastic pricing approach.[48]

Despite these examples, defensive strategies *can* be highly effective. Marshal Henri Petain's successful defence at Verdun (1916) enabled him to put into operation his long-held view that the French Army must fight a defensive war rather than waste men in useless, large-scale attacks. Petain averted the complete collapse of the French Army (1917), did much to restore morale and placed his forces in a position to withstand the German offensives of 1918. Lee Iaccoca rebuilt a shattered Chrysler by adopting a defensive strategy emphasizing cost-effective production techniques based on the use of industrial robots, improved morale which in turn improved quality, closure of inefficient plants, labour force reductions and an effective pricing policy for Chrysler's cars. By mid–1983 Chrysler was in a strong defensive position, able to withstand the competitive situation in the US car market and was again profitable.[49]

The fact remains, that defensive strategies can lead to an excessive reliance on well prepared positions which can prove a delusion and a snare for the unwary. The single–mindedness of a defensive strategy may produce the excuse for an indefinite postponement of the offence. Napoleon described the art of war as 'a well reasoned and extremely circumspect defence, followed by a rapid and audacious attack' — a maxim equally applicable to business combat.

Sound defensive strategies are essential since market leadership is ephemeral. In market as well as military conflict, maintaining a position can be infinitely more difficult than getting there in the first place. Unfortunately, business, while extensively planning offensive actions frequently adopts a reactive approach to competitive threats. While looking down the barrel of a competitor's gun can concentrate the mind remarkably this goes against the fundamental rules of conflict that complacency kills and no–one ever offers a second chance.

Source References

1. The Economist, June 5, 1982.

2. Fortune, November 16, 1981.

3. The Economist, February 14, 1981.

4. Fortune, October 20, 1980.

5. Business Europe, March 20, 1981.

6. McKinsey Quarterly, Spring, 1981.

7. Fortune, June 1, 1981.

8. Business Week, June 29, 1981.

9. Business Week, March 4, 1981.

10. Business Week, June 8, 1981 and The Economist, June 9, 1984.

11.   The Economist, April 10, 1982.

12.   Fortune, June 15, 1981.

13.   Esquire, February, 1980.

14.   McKinsey Quarterly, Winter, 1983.

15.   The Economist, September 26, 1981.

16.   Fortune, June 1, 1981.

17.   Fortune, June 15, 1981.

18.   Business Week, August 24, 1981 and Time, August 13, 1984.

19.   Fortune, April 16, 1981.

20.   Forbes, October 26, 1981.

21.   New York Times, October 4, 1981.

22.   The Economist, June 5, 1982.

23.   Business Week, August 18, 1980.

24.   Business Week, December 17, 1979.

25.   Time, July 19, 1982.

26.   The Economist, July 19, 1980.

27.   The Financial Times, July 8, 1982.

28.   Business Week, December 15, 1980.

29.   Busines Week, February 2, 1982.

30.   The Economist, September 20, 1980.

31.   The Financial Times, April 23,1982.

32.   International Herald Tribune, April 13, 1982.

33.   The Wall Street Journal, June 10, 1982.

34.   The Economist, September 26, 1981.

35.   Fortune, March 23, 1981.

36.   The Wall Street Journal, May 11, 1981.

37.   Fortune, December 1, 1981.

38.   The Wall Street Journal, February 12, 1981.

39.   Time, December 21, 1981.

40.   Business Week, January 26, 1981.

41.   Fortune, August 10, 1981.

42.   The Wall Street Journal, April 13, 1982.

43.   The Economist, May 3, 1980.

44. Fortune, October 19, 1981.
45. Business Week, August 24, 1981.
46. The Economist, February 4, 1984.
47. Esquire, February, 1980.
48. The Wall Street Journal, October 9, 1981.
49. Newsweek, August 2, 1983.

chapter six
ALLIANCE

'Alliances are held together by fear, not by love'.

Harold Macmillan (1959)

Military history is dominated by the use of alliances of two or more combatants against enemies. Alliances have frequently changed the face of history; Blücher's assistance to Wellington at Waterloo (1815) at a critical point in the engagement turned the tide for the Seventh Coalition and led to the final defeat of Napoleon.

The basic object of a military alliance is to combine the forces of actual or potential combatants to overwhelm opponents or to dissuade potential belligerents from conducting a conflict. In war, alliances are built by defenders in response to attack. The alliance of the Allied Powers in World War II was a result of the Japanese pre-emptive strike against Pearl Harbor in December 1941 and the German attack on Russia in June, 1941. Both the USA and Russia then allied themselves with the UK, which had been at war since September 1939, and with China against the Axis alliance of Germany, Italy and Japan.

Under conditions of armed neutrality, alliances are forged to provide a joint response in case of an attack on one or more of the members of the alliance. NATO and the Warsaw Pact are current examples of military alliances based on armed neutrality. Military alliances are based on a commonality of interest between the members of the alliance and are predominantly related to economic, political or religious objectives. The alliances forged by the Hanseatic League in the 14th and 15th centuries were basically economic alliances; the alliances which took place in the English Civil War (1642—1651) were largely supportive of the political differences between Charles I on the one hand and Parliament on the other, while the alliances in the Thirty-Years war (1618—1648) were religious alliances between the Catholic states of Bavaria,

Spain and the Holy Roman Emperor Ferdinand II.

Alliances depend on the ability of the members to sustain their commitment to that alliance. For example, a member of an alliance may be weakened to the extent that it can no longer continue as an active member. Austria's decisive defeat at the battle of Austerlitz in 1805 so weakened that country that it fell out of the Third Coalition with Britain and Russia against Napoleon which delayed Napoleon's final defeat to 1815 at the Battle of Waterloo.

Also military alliances can be weakened by changing interests of the partners. Germany and Russia, for example, formed an alliance to invade Poland in 1939 but were at war with each other in 1941.

In business, alliances are common combat strategies which are formed to serve common interests such as preserving the balance of market power, controlling spheres of influence, and protecting the corporate interests of firms. These alliances combine financial, marketing, production or technological resources in such a way as to serve the common objective (see Figure 6.1).

The early business alliances were cartels or trusts where companies sought means to cut the costs of competition and share in the rewards of a stable market. Typical examples were, in the late 19th century, the Standard Oil Trusts and in the early part of the 20th century, the truly international maze of cartels for a range of chemical products, encompassing I.G. Farben (Germany), ICI (UK), Montecatini (Italy), Aussiger Verein (Czechoslovakia), Boruta (Poland), Mitsui (Japan), and Standard Oil of New Jersey, Du Pont and Dow Chemical (of the US). Two large-scale international cartels are still in existence. De Beers Consolidated Mines produces one third of the world's diamonds and through a complex cartel, the Central Selling Organization (CSO), controls 80% of all diamond sales including those of the USSR. IATA monitors rates and sets standards of service for the majority of airlines on most international flights.

Both the CSO and IATA successfully repelled attempts in the late 1970s to usurp their alliances. The CSO ran into trouble in the late 1970s as a growing number of people bought diamonds as investments. The CSO placed hefty surcharges on larger, higher quality diamonds to discourage the trend; however, the investment diamonds were dumped back on the market to compete with CSO sales. In 1977—1978 the Israelis took advantage of the situation and

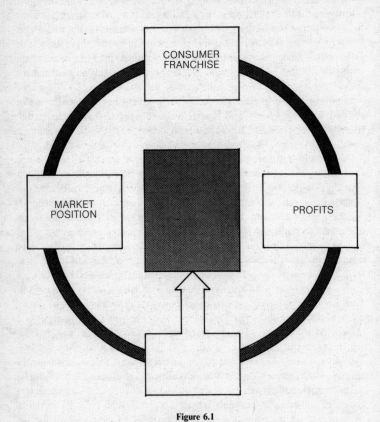

Figure 6.1
BUSINESS ALLIANCES
To preserve market power, control spheres of interest and protect corporate interests.

attempted to break the grip of the CSO; however, the attack was successfully countered and the effort almost broke the Israeli diamond cutting industry.

IATA almost ceased to exist as a cohesive force in the airline market when faced with Freddie Laker's successful legal battle to open regularly scheduled discounted air services across the Atlantic. Some carriers temporarily left the alliance due to the failure of IATA to counter Laker-type threats while US carriers left IATA as a result of the US Government's opposition to the cartel. Following Laker's demise in early 1982, the alliance came back into its own. To avoid falling foul of anti-trust legislation the focus of business alliances has moved away from cartels towards more limited aims.

There are many forms of business alliances (see Table 6.1).

LICENSING
— Where a company grants to another the rights (and technical know-how)to manufacture, distribute and sell a product or service in a specific country or countries for a certain period of time.

Pilkington of the UK widely licensed its float-glass technology in the early 1960s to 16 major foreign glass manufacturers rather than attempt to enter a number of large markets with the initial high capital costs of building large-scale production facilities and distribution systems. By using alliance strategies Pilkington was able to generate the funds for expanding UK domestic production, increasing exports and developing manufacturing capacity in countries such as Argentina, Australia, Canada, India, New Zealand and South Africa which lacked local plate glass production. By the 1970s Pilkington's float-glass technology had almost completely superseded plate glass processes and was into the thick sheet glass market. In 1970 Pilkington's license revenue from its float-glass process was responsible for well over a third of the company's profits.

During the mid-1960s Grundig and Philips introduced competing but incompatible audio cassette systems in Europe. Philips took the offensive by widely licensing the system to other electronic consumer goods manufacturers who would be future competitors to Philips' own cassette recorders and players. The widespread availability and popularity of the audio-cassette medium forced Grundig, who had not licensed-out its own system, to quickly obtain a license for the Philips system which had become the

Licensing

Marketing Agreements /Dual Marketing

Joint Ventures

Franchising

Private Label

Buyer–Seller

Consortia

Common Standards

Research Alliances

Technology/Market Access

Table 6.1
KEY ALLIANCE STRATEGIES

industry standard. In the mid-1970s Sony introduced a larger cassette system, Elcaset. However, Sony did not pursue a vigorous licensing strategy and Elcaset has remained a low volume product limited to a few Sony cassette players.

BL, with its market share eroding and in a precarious financial situation, had neither the cash nor engineering resources to develop a medium-sized car to replace the ageing Dolomite, as a strategy to generate showroom traffic and rebuild its European dealer network. Instead BL reached a licensing agreement with Honda to manufacture the Acclaim for sale in the EEC markets with Honda supplying engines, gearboxes and auxiliary equipment.[1]

ICL, the largest European-owned manufacturer of data processing equipment, needed to rejuvenate its product line to compete in fast growing segments of the market. ICL concluded an agreement with Three Rivers of the US to manufacture and market the latter's powerful Perq microcomputer outside the USA. ICL's strategy was to form an alliance with another manufacturer who could supply skills and products deficient at ICL. In exchange, ICL offered its extensive world-wide marketing network and its technological and development engineering talents.[2] ICL has also licensed PABX switch products from Mitel of Canada to round out its office automation line as a strategy to serve large customers with a portfolio of products and services.

Anheuser-Busch's Budweiser beer by 1981 had become the second largest selling imported beer in Japan after Heineken. The licensing deal with a large Japanese brewer, Suntory, in 1981 was designed to drop the price of Budweiser, then selling at twice the price of local Japanese beers, through a local brewing arrangement which enabled Budweiser to increase sales volume by overcoming its price disadvantage.[3]

By astute licensing-out of technology, licensors can also gain a measure of control over the use to which the technology is put, the markets where it is sold and its price, to avoid the spectre of the firm competing with itself. RCA's failure to provide such safeguards on its colour television technology license to the Japanese in the 1950s, enabled the Japanese electronics manufacturers to decimate the US colour TV market in the late 1960s and 1970s. Licensing-out also provides the licensor with the ability to deflect the licensee from developing a competitive product. Pilkington's wide licensing-out of its float-glass technology to the sixteen major world plate glass manufacturers in the early 1960s forestalled much larger companies from developing competitive technology to rival Pilkington's process and enabled the company, through large licensing fees, to become a major force in its own right.

MARKETING AGREEMENTS

— These usually involve the host company taking on the sales management of products or services from the initiator — the company new to the market. It is not a license agreement since the host company is not given rights to patented know-how, nor is it a joint venture since it does not involve a capital agreement nor the creation of a jointly owned company. A recent example of a marketing agreement is Renault's agreement with American Motors (AMC) where Renault markets its cars through AMC's 1,700 strong dealer network in the USA.[4]

Rather than directly market the ZX-81 personal computer in Japan for reasons of market size, distribution complexity and cost, Sinclair Research concluded a marketing agreement with one of Japan's largest trading companies, Mitsui, to market the ZX-81 in Japan.[5] By late 1981, the US semiconductor industry was facing a situation where profit margins were shrinking, the cost of integrated circuit development was spiralling and technical manpower shortages were becoming apparent. Intel, one of the largest firms, and Advanced Micro Devices (AMD) signed a 10-year agreement covering marketing, cross-licensing and technology exchange, primarily to fend off increased Japanese competition and offer a second source of supply for domestic customers.[6]

A variation on the marketing agreement is dual marketing where the same product is marketed by two companies under different trade marks. Glaxo, a medium-sized UK pharmaceutical company, developed an advanced anti-ulcer drug, ranitidine, but was faced with a formidable financial and marketing task in the US where the $400 million anti-ulcer market was created and dominated by Smith Kline Beckman and where Glaxo had a limited market presence with its own small marketing subsidiary. In 1983 Glaxo forged a dual marketing alliance with the much larger Hoffmann-La Roche to market ranitidine to support its own marketing efforts.

JOINT VENTURES

— Which generally involve the legal establishment of a jointly owned subsidiary.

A joint venture strategy was used successfully by Syntex and Astra to market the former's pharmaceutical products in Scandinavia. Joint ventures can also involve R&D activities which, when completed, leave the partners free to carry out independent marketing. Hoffmann–La Roche and Burroughs–Wellcome jointly developed the anti–infective drug trimethoprin and each partner vigorously competed under different trademarks.

Maisons Pheñix, a French company specializing in inexpensive prefabricated homes, entered the US market in 1981 through a joint venture with US Home Corporation. Maisons Pheñix, already the largest home builder in Europe, sought a new market and US Home, the largest American home builder, needed capital to buy land for more housing tract development. Maisons Pheñix imported its own technology, manufacturing process, cash, management and marketing approach, providing a new product and concept in home building and marketing by door–to–door sales, while US Home provided the corporate structure and land for development.[7]

One of the most durable and successful joint ventures is that of Scandinavian Airlines System (SAS). At the end of the Second World War the national flag carriers of Denmark (Det Danske Luftfartselskab), Norway (Det Norsk Luftruter) and Sweden (Svensk Interkontinental Lufttrafik) realized that they could not individually finance major aircraft re–equipment programmes and open up world–wide airline routes in competition with airlines from countries with much larger economic resources. In 1946 the three companies established a multi–national flag carrier owned two-sevenths each by DDL and DNL and three–sevenths by SILA with the monopoly on international and domestic trunk routes. The new airline, operational in 1948, has become a significant factor in the world air transport market — a position which none of the individual members could have attained independently.

FRANCHISING
— Where trademarks, know–how, exclusivity and management assistance are provided for a down–payment, royalties and compliance with company standards.

Following the American Civil War (1861—1865) Singer Sewing Machines was one of the first firms to establish an international distribution system by franchising dealers. In the 1960s franchising expanded across a wide range of industries, particularly in the USA. Accounting and tax counselling services (H & R Block), car exhaust systems (Midas Muffler) and transmissions (AAMCO), garden care services (Lawn Doctor), employment agencies (Kelly), fast food outlets (Baskin–Robbins, Dunkin' Donuts, Kentucky Fried Chicken, McDonalds and Pizza Hut), pharmacies (Rexall), real estate agents (Century 21) and unfinished furniture (Naked Furniture) are some applications of large–scale franchising operations in the US. In many countries oil companies have franchised petrol stations. Avis built its international car rental operations largely on franchising, the operations of the Hilton International Hotel chain outside the USA are based on a form of franchising and Sodima, a french food company, has franchised its Yoplait yoghurt in 35 countries.

PRIVATE LABEL ALLIANCES
— Where one company manufacturers a product for sale under the brand name of another. Such alliances have been in existence from the turn of the century.

Initially packaged food was the staple private label business. Tesco in the UK is an example of a retail outlet contracting out the processing and packaging of food products sold under its trademark while Migros in Switzerland has integrated backwards into the production of products for sale in Migros–owned outlets. Marks & Spencer (mini–department stores) in the UK and Sears, Roebuck (full line department stores) in the US are retail outlets who have built substantial businesses devoted to the sale of products produced by other companies for sale under the retail outlets' house brand names. More recently firms in Japan, South Korea and Taiwan have supplied television sets, cars, audio equipment and computers to European and US firms through private label contracts for sale under the latter firm's brand names.

SELLER–BUYER ALLIANCES
— Where the level of success for both seller and buyer is dependent on co–operative participation, where the efforts of either party support those of the other. Such alliances frequently occur in large–scale manufacturing projects, and where one component of the product may have a critical impact on a key success factor such as cost, packaging or distribution.

General Dynamics in selling the F-16 fighter to Belgium, Denmark, Holland and Norway reached agreements which offset purchase costs against local manufacture of components and partial assembly in all four countries. Northrop in a $400 million contract with Switzerland for F-5E fighters agreed to market $135 million of Swiss products world-wide. This involved Northrop marketing shelving material to Saudi Arabia, drilling machines to Spain, water filtration equipment systems to Morocco and transport boats to Bolivia.[8]

Other seller-buyer alliances include technology. For example, Tetra-Pak of Sweden developed asceptic packaging which provides major cost reduction benefits in packaging, shipping and storage over bottles and cans. Following the US Food and Drug Administration's approval in 1981 a number of companies, including Borden, Coca-Cola, Dairymen and Ocean Spray, began putting asceptic packages into US supermarkets at lower costs than products in conventional bottles or cans allowing them to undercut competitors.

CONSORTIUM ALLIANCES

— Alliances have also developed on a consortium basis where the cost of competing is extremely high and one company alone cannot fund the costs of development, manufacturing and marketing.

Typical examples have been in major public construction programmes such as roads, bridges and dams. However, more recently consortia have been formed to tackle high risk and high cost projects. Airbus Industrie was formed from a consortium of French, German, Dutch, British, Spanish and Italian aerospace manufacturers to finance, design, build and sell the A300 and A310 Airbus aircraft. The BWR consortium of GEC, Hitachi, ASEA and Toshiba was formed to develop atomic reactors. Racal has used consortia to sell packaged military electronics systems; and the offshore oil and gas exploration programs in the North Sea and in the Yellow Sea have been largely operated on a consortium basis.

COMMON STANDARDS ALLIANCE

— Alliances have also been based on common standards.

During the late 1970s, the European computer industry attempted an alliance strategy against IBM and the Japanese manufacturers to stop them from gaining complete dominance of the European market for mainframe computers. An attempt was made to establish common standards for all European data processing equipment in order to gain the economies of scale which IBM and Japanese manufacturers enjoyed. In addition, the French company, CH–Honeywell Bull, developed an architecture for a distributed system that enabled different makers' equipment to 'talk' to each other on digital networks. The design was offered to other European computer makers if they would agree to adopt the system as a standard. This would have forced IBM, already with its own standard, to modify all of its equipment for Europe or be frozen out of substantial markets.[9]

RESEARCH ALLIANCES

— Research alliances have also been formed with the object of combining resources to fund high cost, long range research for major technological innovation.

Miti in Japan is co–ordinating the JIPDEC program for long range research projects in advanced computer sciences, including computers with artificial intelligence and supercomputers designed to outflank the US computer industry's supremacy. As a counter move eighteen US computer and semiconductor companies including Control Data, Honeywell, Motorola and RCA joined a non–profit research co–operative, MCC, to pool resources and share the costs of long range research for the fifth generation computer which will include new architecture, software and artificial intelligence. The results of MCC's research will be used exclusively by the sponsors for three years.

TECHNOLOGY AND MARKET ACCESS ALLIANCES

— Alliance strategies centred on technology and market access have proliferated in the last few years.

In the case of technology, Japanese companies seek access to western product innovation. For example, Mitsubishi's joint venture with Armco is designed to obtain access to the latter's lightweight plastic composites by selling and later manufacturing in Japan. Western companies in turn seek access to low cost Japanese manufacturing technology. Bendix, for example, has a joint venture with Muraza to produce Bendix machine tools in Japan for sale in the US, at 75% of the cost of the same products manufactured in the USA.

In the case of market access, western companies seek local

alliances to penetrate the tightly controlled Japanese market–place by linking up with established Japanese companies with local manufacturing, distribution and marketing skills. Volkswagen's co-operative manufacturing and marketing agreement with Nissan is centred around Nissan producing Volkswagen's Santana car for sale in Japan. VW supplies 30% of the Santana parts direct from Germany and Nissan, with 70% local parts sourcing, assembles the Santana in Japan. By the end of June 1984 10,000 Santanas had been sold in Japan compared with 17,000 in the whole of Europe in 1983, illustrating the value of such alliances.[10] Japanese companies faced with a rising level of European and US protectionism are seeking political insurance through link–ups with powerful local companies. Toyota's arrangement with General Motors to jointly produce small Toyota–designed cars in a $300 million refitted factory in California, and Fujitsu's co–operative product development and marketing arrangement with Siemens and ICL for mainframe computers in Western Europe and with Amdahl in the USA, are typical recent examples.[11]

There are a large number of variations on these basic alliance strategies in business. For example, the French car manufacturers in 1979 and 1980 were using a range of alliance strategies to cut costs, expand the scale of various production facilities, tie into advanced technology and geographically expand their operations. In December 1979 Renault agreed to design a new car in collaboration with Volvo of Sweden and purchased 10% of Volvo's equity. Renault increased its holding in AMC to 46% in September 1980 and planned to build a mid–sized car in AMC's Kenosha plant. Peugeot and Fiat of Italy combined production and sales facilities in Argentina in February 1980 and agreed to design and build an electronic engine later in the year. In addition to these strategies Renault and Peugeot formed an alliance to produce engines and gearboxes in France.[12]

The mutuality of interest is an important business alliance issue and is well illustrated by the agreement between Ajinimoto of Japan and Searle of the USA concerning Aspartame, a natural low calorie sweetener that has become a major competitor to saccharine. Ajinimoto, the world's largest manufacturer of the seasoning, monosodium glutamate, recognized the huge potential of an exclusive supply agreement with Searle for Aspartame as a replacement for saccharine, initially as a table–top sweetener but

also for use in the manufacture of instant teas and coffees,
beverages, mixes, pre-sweetened cereals, chewing-gum, dry gelatine
and dairy toppings. Searle on the other hand, counted on
Ajinimoto's advanced technology in amino acids to produce
Aspartame at low cost to provide the margins necessary to penetrate
the market dominated by saccharine.[13]

The key to an effective business alliance is the capability of the
partners to sustain commitment. The joint venture between Ampex
and Toshiba in Japan to produce magnetic tape and videotape
recorders, for example, collapsed due to a major difference of
opinion between the partners on how to restructure the deficit-
ridden operation.

SUMMARY

Alliances in business are used as strategies to preserve the balance
of market power, to control spheres of influence and protect the
corporate interests of firms through armed neutrality, to deter
potential competitors, or to attack or defend market positions.
Companies in traditional industries such as cars, farm machinery,
steel and tyres, tend to look for alliances which take up spare
capacity, while those in high technology industries form alliances to
break into new markets.

As in war, companies are only one set of actors on the battlefield
and other actors including consumer groups, governments and
supra-national agencies have the power and influence to override
or seriously modify manœuvres designed to lower the perceived
level of competition. Social controls imposed by consumer interests
and legal constraints dictated by governments and surpa-national
agencies, all have the capability to control market activity and
prevent accretions of power and the abuse of market position.
Although business alliances have moved from cartels towards more
limited aims in specific circumstances to avoid falling foul of
growing pro-competitive law, the wider interpretations placed on
anti-trust legislation by many governments have placed some limit
on the use of business alliance strategies. Relationships with
competitors, suppliers and customers, and licensing agreements
have frequently been interpreted as anti-competitive by
governments.

Alliance strategies have a number of drawbacks in business.

There are great difficulties in tracking the experience gained, accountability is slack, communications are weak, decisions take too long and are often tackled in an ad hoc fashion — all of which can cause severe operating problems. For example; the Tornado multi-role combat aircraft (MRCA) produced in an alliance between British Aerospace, MBB and Aeritalia went well over budget; the collaborative agreement to produce the System X telecommunications project developed by British Telecom with GEC and Plessey suffered considerable technical delays; and the BMW–Steyr–Daimler–Puch project to manufacture diesel engines in Austria was abandoned. Temporary alliances to protect long-term independence may weaken rather than strengthen a company's abilities, since they can lose the capacity and capability to produce a fully integrated product in the future. The British Aerospace collaboration to make wings for Airbus Industrie has probably placed BAe in a position where it has lost the staff, experience, and finance to build an Airbus-sized civil aircraft project on its own in the future. Proprietory information can easily flow to allies and a partner may become too dependent on a collaborator for essential components.[14]

Both the military and business depend heavily on the use of alliance strategies in modern combat for essentially the same reasons. The rising cost of battlefield and market conflict, the need to match competitive resource deployment and the global nature of conflict require effective alliance strategies for both survival and growth. Business alliances are short lived since they are designed to meet a specific threat and a common interest between the partners is difficult to sustain over time and as conditions change. Any company relying totally on an alliance as the core strategy, without developing an independent strategic approach for future use or as a contingency, is at risk when circumstances change. When McDonalds' relationship with a French franchisee, Dayan, collapsed over a standards dispute, McDonalds was faced with a major competitive challenge from its former ally. Dayan converted its fourteen well-located McDonalds restaurants in Paris overnight to the O'Kitch hamburger chain, forcing McDonalds to start from scratch in a market where the fast food hamburger was approaching saturation. With no independent strategic approach, McDonalds was completely vulnerable to Dayan's switch from an ally to a competitor in France.

Source References

1. The Financial Times, October 7, 1981.

2. The Financial Times, September 16, 1981.

3. Business Week, June 19, 1981.

4. Business Week, October 13, 1980.

5. The Financial Times, October 23, 1981.

6. Business Week, October 19, 1981.

7. The Wall Street Journal, October 16, 1981.

8. Time, October 26, 1981.

9. Business Week, December 17, 1979.

10. Business Week, August 6, 1984

11. The Wall Street Journal, May 18, 1983.

12. Business Week, October 13, 1981.

13. Business Week, September 29, 1980.

14. The Economist, February 11, 1984.

chapter seven

COMBAT SUPPORT

> 'Nine times out of ten an army has been destroyed because its supply
> lines have been severed'.
>
> > General Douglas MacArthur (1950)

Effective weaponry, access to information on the enemy's positions
and intentions, the effective organization and leadership of combat
groups, efficient communications and adequate supplies, are the
key resources of any army or company in conflict (see Figure 7.1).
Unless these resources are used to effectively support the army or
company, and are qualitatively and quantitatively superior to those
of the enemy, strategies cannot be implemented or executed
successfully.

   This chapter focuses on the five key support elements used in
military and business conflict (see Table 7.1).

WEAPONRY

'A Weapon is defensive or offensive depending on which end of it is
pointing at you'.

> > Premier Aristide Briand (1930)

The introduction of new weapons has had a major impact on both
the outcome of individual battles and on the conduct of warfare
throughout history. Weapons have been used to gain both tactical
battlefield advantage and to conduct warfare strategically.

TACTICAL WEAPONRY
The longbow, originally a Welsh weapon, was adopted by the
English and became a devastating force virtually throughout the
Hundred Years War between England and France. Battles from
Crecy (1346) to Agincourt (1415) were won largely by the effective
use of the longbow. Although the first recorded use of a gun in

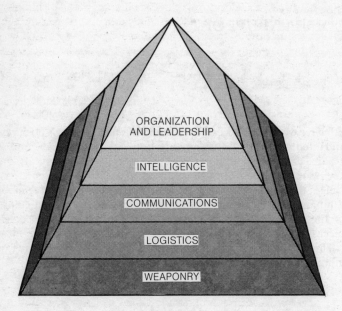

Figure 7.1
COMBAT SUPPORT ELEMENTS

Key business resources — weaponry, intelligence, communications, logistics, and organization and leadership.

European warfare was in 1324 at Metz, field artillery began to affect the shape of war almost a century later in the second half of the Hundred Years War. The effective use of field artillery by Henry V at the siege of Harfleur (1415) signalled the end of the era of the impregnable fortress. The machine-gun originally developed in Belgium in the 1850s, improved by Gatling (1862), was finally perfected by Maxim in 1882 and, with modifications, became the Vickers gun used in both 1914—1918 and 1939—1945 world wars. Montgomery suggests that probably more than any other weapon it was responsible for the character of trench warfare, and probably no other type of weapon killed so many soldiers.

STRATEGIC WEAPONRY

The submarine, invented by Brun (1863) and developed into semi-submersibles by the Confederate forces in the American Civil War (1861—1865) was used with devastating effect by the German Kriegsmarine in both the 1914—1918 and 1939—1945 wars as a strategic weapon. In 1917 and again in 1942—1943, the U-Boats almost severed the flow of raw materials and food necessary for Britain to continue to wage war. The aircraft-carrier, although conceived during the First World War, became a major strategic weapon in the 1939—1945 war since it provided mobile bases for offensive and defensive air power. The strategic defeats of the Japanese carrier forces at the battles of Coral Sea (1942), which prevented the invasion of Australia, and Midway (1942), which inflicted crippling carrier losses on the Japanese from which they were never to recover, marked the turning point of the war in the Pacific Theatre. The use of bombers was successfully demonstrated by the Germans against Britain in 1917—1918 and although defeated in the Battle of Britain (1940), emerged as an effective long-range strategic weapon in the hands of the Americans and British over Germany (1942—1945).

The value of weaponry is time-limited since an enemy can develop counter weapons and duplicate weaponry. Plate armour had so improved by 1450, that longbow-men were becoming obsolete. Radar, fighter aircraft, anti-aircraft guns and later missiles, were developed to counter strategic bombers; and convoys, anti-submarine radar, heat-seeking devices, long-range patrol aircraft, depth charges, hunter-killer submarines and satellite tracking have been developed to combat submarines. Weapons

1. WEAPONRY

    - Technological
    - Production
    - Financial
    - Marketing

2. INTELLIGENCE

    - Competitive
    - Market
    - Environmental

3. ORGANIZATION AND LEADERSHIP

4. COMMUNICATION

5. LOGISTICS

    - Raw Materials
    - Production
    - Distribution
    - Product Support.

Table 7.1
KEY COMBAT SUPPORT ELEMENTS

used effectively by an adversary have been in turn used even more successfully by the opponent. The tank is a case in point. Repeating his earlier successes in France in 1940 with armour in Russia, Guderian eventually encountered superior Russian armour. Furthermore poison gas attacks used first by the Germans at Ypres in 1915, were met within a few months by gas counter-attacks by the British. Although weaponry has played a significant part in warfare, weapons have not by themselves resulted in strategic victory. Patton makes the analogies that while Julius Ceasar defeated the poorly armed Gauls he did the same to the armed legions of Pompeii, and that while in 1866 Prussia defeated the less well armed Austrians it went on to destroy the better armed French in 1870.

Weaponry is an indispensable part of business combat and four main weapons — technology, production, finance and marketing — are used by companies in market conflict.

Technological Weapons

Technological weapons are used to create entirely new markets, to develop alternatives to competing products, to provide superior customer benefits, and to supply production advantages.

NEW MARKETS

Apple developed and introduced the first personal computer in 1977. Apple's revolutionary product created an entirely new segment in the computer market which grew at a phenomenal rate fuelled by consumer demand and heavy competition. From a few million dollars in sales in 1977 the personal computer market in the US alone was valued at $4.2 billion by 1982 — a direct result of Apple's innovative product.

In the late 1970s Smith Kline Beckman developed and introduced the first effective anti-ulcer drug therapy, the H_2 receptor cimetidine, providing physical relief and cost-effective treatment for patients who had previously been treated non-therapeutically by surgery or diet. Smith Kline Beckman's technological breakthrough in anti-ulcer therapy created a major new segment in the drug market in excess of $1 billion in 1983, which made cimetidine the largest selling drug world-wide.

PRODUCT ALTERNATIVES

Three alternative technologies were developed to compete in the videodisc market — the low cost RCA stylus system, the more expensive MCA/Philips laser-optical videodisc and the Matsushita optical tracking system — none of which will play discs made for the other two.[1]

Using computer technology, Reuters, an international news agency, created an alternative business information system to the telephone and teleprinter services in the early 1970s. The original Reuters Monitor Service had grown from fourteen subscribers in 1973 to 6,200 in 1980, and the initial money market information had been expanded to take in stock market, commodity, and general business news services. By 1983, Reuters' Monitor was offering forty-six domestic money and equity services, and eighteen international market, commodity and news services to 13,000 subscribers on 34,000 monitors in seventy-seven countries, and had all but destroyed the financial community's reliance on the telephone and teleprinter.

CUSTOMER BENEFITS

Wilkinson's polymer-coated 'Super Sword Edge' razor blades offered significant customer benefits — a closer shave than existing carbon steel razor blades and a lower cost per shave — which quickly converted the market-place to the new technology.

Sony's innovative Walkman, an ultra-small audio-cassette tape player, offered significant customer advantages in terms of size, weight, sound quality and truly self-contained portability over its bulkier, semi-portable rivals, and quickly became the market standard and a major money-spinner for Sony.[2]

PRODUCTION ADVANTAGE

Kaman, a US helicopter manufacturer with an idle repair shop and automated woodworking equipment, used techniques from the aerospace industry such as oscilloscope and vibration tests, and successfully entered the guitar manufacturing business. Kaman developed an improved guitar made of spruce which took 2 man-hours to produce against 20 man-hours for other makers. In 1981 Kaman's Ovation line of guitars were the best selling acoustic guitars with over 75% of the US market. Kaman's success in an entirely new type of business was determined largely by the application of new technology which provided significant pro-duction advantages.[3]

Production Weapons

The production weapon is used in quality, quantity and cost battles with competitors.

QUALITY WEAPONS

Maytag has been able to lead the US washing machine market for years at a 15% premium over its nearest competitor, General Electric. It successfully weathered the US recession as a result of its reputation for reliability and durability and was able to maintain volume in a declining market. Similarly the quality weapon was an integral feature of the successful Japanese penetrations of both the US imported car market and the market for 4K and 16K random access memory (RAM) chips in the US.[4]

QUANTITY WEAPONS

Texas Instrument's use of the Experience Curve strategy   a volume weapon in conjunction with progressive cost and price declines — continuously opened up new market segments and enabled TI to dominate the market for personal calculators by 1977 — five years after its entry into the market.[5] Hoffmann–La Roche's productive capacity for ascorbic acid, or vitamin C, is such that it can outproduce the rest of its competitors combined; this enables Roche to use capacity as a weapon to counter price attacks on its 60% share of the world market for Vitamin C.

COST WEAPONS

Part of the reason for Toyota's phenomenal success in the car market has been its unique cost-effective production strategy. Toyota's Kanban system of car assembly calls for daily delivery of the exact number of components from outside suppliers at specific points on the assembly line. The Kanban system provided Toyota with the ability to cut inventory costs by transferring stockholdings to suppliers and minimized downtime by ensuring component delivery in the right order, at the right time at the right place in the assembly process. The Kanban system gave Toyota a significant cost advantage.[6]

The Japanese steel producers realised that they could not obtain a meaningful share of the world market by relying on imported raw materials and high energy costs. They identified a new oxygen process developed by an obscure Austrian steel mill and, despite a long development period and high investment costs, the oxygen process provided the Japanese steel makers with a massive cost advantage. The resulting high quality steel at the lowest world cost enabled the Japanese to dominate the world steel market.

Financial Weapons

Financial weapons are used tactically to secure short-term advantages and strategically to weaken competitors over time.

TACTICAL WEAPONS

Finance is used to fund tactical campaigns emphasizing price, promotion and credit attacks on competitors. Introductory offers, discounting, coupons, sampling, selective price cuts, promotional allowances and quantity discounts are all financial weapons designed to penetrate, hold and increase share against competitors.

During an eight month period in 1982 Chesebrough-Ponds flooded the $600 million US spaghetti sauce market with $60 million worth of cents-off coupons to maintain and expand Ragu's commanding 53% share of the market. This tactic played havoc with competitive brand loyalty as the typical coupon offer, 40 cents, was often doubled by supermarkets, prompting non-Ragu users to switch to Ragu to obtain the significant price savings.[7]

Faced with a loss of market leadership to Philip Morris and the decline in the US cigarette market due to rising local, state and federal excise taxes, R.J. Reynolds introduced its Century Regular and Lights brands. Century was launched in 1983 in packs of 25, 20% more than the conventional pack, but retailed at the same price. The de facto 20% price reduction for Century was an innovative financial strategy designed to attack both Philip Morris and meet the increasing value consciousness of consumers faced with rising taxes which had pushed retail prices beyond $1 per pack. By mid 1984 Century had won an 0.7% share of the US cigarette market making it the most successful new product introduced by Reynolds since 1976.[8]

Procter & Gamble uses its $500 million annual promotional budget as a tactical financial weapon to fight off companies attempting to enter, or increase share in P&G markets. Colgate-Palmolive after many years of being dominated by P&G in almost half its business in the US, diversified in the 1970s into markets away from P&G where Colgate was less vulnerable to the pressures of P&G's promotional strength.[9]

Easy credit terms are used as a tactical financial weapon to induce purchase and to offset prices in the European mail order business which are often higher than those charged by retail outlets.[10]

In large mature industries where companies have huge fixed costs such as airlines, hotels, television, shipping and film-making, one percentage point in sales can bring in millions in additional profits. Since the cost to supply and sell additional product or service are relatively low in comparison to the fixed costs, financial muscle is frequently used as a tactical weapon to fund short-run saturation promotion to gain profitable market share gains.

STRATEGIC WEAPONS

BIC's low-cost disposable ballpoint pens, lighters and razors have all been marketed using the financial strategy of absorbing several years of heavy losses incurred by intensive promotion to penetrate the market and build a large market share which will bring future profits through volume.[11]

Xerox used finance as a strategic weapon to build an early position defence around its photocopier business. By leasing rather than selling photocopiers, Xerox forced its early competitors to either fund the large amounts of working capital necessary for a large-scale leasing operation or to avoid the market.

Merrill Lynch, Wall Street's largest brokerage house, launched its Cash Management Account (CMA) in 1977 as a strategic financial weapon to lure new business away from banks and other brokerage houses. The CMA is a brokerage account with a cheque book and a Visa Card. However, loose cash in the account earns high interest in a money market fund. The mixture of ready cash and high interest rates drew business from customers who would have normally used a regular bank which under US banking regulations could not pay market-related rates of interest, and away from other brokerage houses.

The CMA was for many years a loss-leader designed to lure business into Merrill Lynch, however with more than one million CMA accounts with balances of more than $70 billion in 1984 the CMA became a profit centre in its own right.[12]

Marketing Weapons

Marketing weapons are a set of tactical and strategic weapons used to enhance the opportunities provided by technological, production and financial weapons.

TACTICAL WEAPONS

Differentiating a product from competition is the most widely used tactical marketing weapon. The fast setting nature of cyanoacrylate, or instant glue, makes the products very hard to handle. Loctite stole a lead on its competitors by introducing a pen–like dispenser which neatly applied a drop of glue when the point was depressed. Loctite's unique packaging was a significant customer benefit since it made the glue easier and less hazardous to use and enabled Loctite to take market leadership.[13]

Singapore Airlines (SIA) was faced with considerable difficulties in securing profitable operations with limited resources against strong international competition. Since SIA was obliged to charge the same fare structures as its competitors to gain route access SIA elected not to joint IATA and was able to use superior service as a tactical weapon to differentiate its product and gain market share. SIA offered higher standards of passenger service in all classes and in tourist class pioneered a choice of meals and free headsets and drinks. SIA's tactics were so successful that it rapidly achieved high load factors against established competitors and, in its early operations, was often not able to meet the demand for seats.

The high price of meat forced McDonald's to use price as a tactical weapon to compete successfully in the Japanese fast food market. To overcome the price disadvantage of the main ingredient of its key product, McDonald's kept the retail price low on the hamburger but increased prices on french fries, soft drinks and desserts. By switching profit emphasis to the 'accessories' which are invariably purchased with hamburgers McDonald's was able to overcome the effect of the high price of meat, maintain overall profit levels and achieve mass market volumes.

STRATEGIC WEAPONS

Niche and segmentation techniques are the most important strategic marketing weapons in business conflict. Makita, the Japanese power–tool company succeeded in capturing 20% of the European and US markets by identifying and filling high growth niches for new or improved power–tools and then outmarketing the leader, Black & Decker. Makita introduced a hammer drill in Europe to create a niche not served by Black & Decker and a low–

cost angle grinder in Austria to compete against Black & Decker's higher priced product. Makita pioneered new distribution channels in building supply stores and discount centres while Black & Decker maintained distribution through hardware stores, and while Black & Decker maintained a rigid pricing structure, Makita adopted liberal discounts.[14]

Häagen Daz successfully used a niche strategy to penetrate the $2.3 billion US ice-cream market in the mid-1970s. Häagen Daz developed a rich, natural ingredient, high quality product aimed at an exclusive segment of the market. Häagen Daz' product was able to command a price up to 75% higher than competitive ice-creams through quality and, with a liberal retailer margins policy, Häagen Daz secured rapid distribution with a higher ROI factor than its competitors. Although other high quality brands, such as Alpen Zauber and Frusan Gladjé emerged as competitors, Häagen Daz achieved a growth rate of 25% between 1976 and 1980, while the US ice–cream market grew by a scant 0.4%.

Similarly Flexnit, a high quality US lingerie manufacturer, adopted a niche strategy in the brassiere market. Flexnit identified that 18—20% of American women are 'A' cup, a market relatively neglected by the major manufacturers. Flexnit introduced its A–OK line of brassieres to meet specific consumer needs in the 'A' cup market and secured the niche before other, larger manufacturers, were able to respond to the challenge.[15]

Many companies in the fast–moving consumer goods markets use segmentation by developing a multi–brand and multi–pack size approach to the market. This serves to attack competition on a wide front, produce multiple selling opportunities by reaching a wide range of market segments with similar products, create entry barriers by monopolizing retail shelf space, reduce the risk of a major victory by a new competitor, and limit the damage of a single brand failure. In the UK, Petfoods sell Bounce, Chappie, Chum, Lassie and Pal brands in the dog–food market and Katkins, Kit–E–Kat and Whiskas in the cat–food market in a variety of sizes. All the products are priced differently and promoted individually to appeal to different segments of the market.

Continuous brand segmentation is also used to gain market share over time. From 1965, when Right Guard was launched as the first aerosol deodorant in the UK, Gillette has been using a continuous segmentation approach to the market. In 1969 Right Guard's proven claim of being the most effective deodorant enabled Gillette to gain an 11.5% share of the market. In 1976 Gillette introduced a clothes protection ingredient and pushed Right Guard's share to 17.5% and in 1981, with the launch of an unperfumed product and roll-on format, Right Guard was able to capture 21.6% of the deodorant market and secure brand leadership.

Business weaponry provides only short-term advantages over competition. Counter weapons and duplicate weapons can be developed to offset the tactical and strategic advantages provided by a firm's technological, production, financial or marketing weapons.

The patent system alerts competitors to technological and production innovations and can be used as a basis for developing substitutes or more advanced versions of the original product. In the pharmaceutical industry, the rapid development of the second generation cephalosporin antibiotic drug by a number of companies to compete with the innovators, is an excellent example of the patent system limiting long-term technological advantages through the fixed period of exclusivity and the disclosure of the invention. Microprocessors had been in use for years in many applications and, until the mid-1970s, each microprocessor was pre-programmed for a specific task and the quantities produced for each application were limited. Intel devised a general purpose microprocessor that could be programmed to fit many different applications, thereby permitting mass production and lower costs. Almost immediately Intel's 8080 microprocessor became the industry standard, displacing Intel's competitors who had to scramble to catch up.[16]

Sony introduced the first successful mass-market videotape recorder, Betamax, in early 1975. Matsushita, rarely a product innovator, introduced its competing VHS system a year later. Matsushita's VHS product offered considerable consumer benefits over the Betamax, with a longer playing time of four to six hours versus two hours for the Betamax, in a more compact format, at a 10% to 15% lower price, and with a large selection of pre-recorded films on VHS videotape for sale or rent by third parties to customers. By 1983, Sony's share of the world VTR market had fallen to below 30% from 68% in 1979, and Sony's major Japanese licensees, NEC, Toshiba and Sanyo, and Zenith, the largest US licensee, had all fully or partially defected to Matsushita's rival VHS system which had become, with around 70% of the world market, the dominant VTR system.

Changing conditions can also alter the value of technological weaponry. In the US chemical industry during the 1970s, when the market for synthetics matured and opportunities for substitution for other materials ran out, the ability to hold down production costs replaced technological prowess as the key success factor in the industry. DuPont lost its leadership to Dow Chemicals which foresaw the change and concentrated on finding low cost sources for its raw material needs. Wilkinson revolutionized the wet-shave market with its innovative polymer-coated 'Super Sword Edge' blades in the mid-1960s which offered consumer benefits in the form of a closer shave than carbon steel blades. However, Gillette was able to counter the threat to its 60% share of the world wet-shave market within 18 months with its own stainless steel blades and outproduced Wilkinson who could not match the scale of Gillette's world-wide productive resources. Within 4 months of its new product launch Gillette had re-secured 57% of the world wet-shave market.

Production advantages can be learned and applied effectively by competitors. Texas Instruments applied its experience curve strategy, which it had used so effectively in the electronic calculator market, to its 99 range of home computers, dropping price progressively from over $950 in 1981 to $100 in 1983. Atari, Commodore and Mattel quickly followed the same strategy with their own home computers, with Commodore actually beating TI on costs, which offset TI's cost and price advantage. A component failure in early 1983, cost $28 million to rectify and led to a loss of customer confidence reflected in a fall in the 99 's market share which was compounded by TI's experience curve approach. TI withdrew from the market in late 1983, writing off $330 million to close down its home computer business.[17]

Financial advantages can change rapidly. Retail outlets, for example, learned to compete on credit terms with the mail order business and furthermore, during the summer of 1980, retail outlets in France, Germany and the UK lowered prices further reducing the appeal of mail order catalogues.[18] Canon developed an alternative process to xerography for plain paper copying, used microprocessor technology to develop small, typewriter-sized, copiers and later, fast copying and colour machines, which enabled Canon to push desk copiers directly against Xerox and overcome Xerox' financial strategy of leasing photocopiers. Canon, backed by heavy promotion and competitive prices, achieved 20% of the Japanese copier market behind Ricoh but ahead of Xerox and, by 1979, had attained 10% of the copier installations in the US.

Marketing weapons can also convey limited advantage. Following Loctite's unique packaging of instant glue, competitors rapidly developed similar packing, reducing Loctite's exclusivity and ultimately market share.[19] BIC's entrance into the US wet-shave market with a new shave concept, offering a complete plastic razor for the price of a conventional blade, forced the market leader Gillette to react in 1976 with a twin-bladed disposable razor. By 1980 Gillette's disposables, backed by a massive promotional campaign, had captured 12% of the wet-shave business compared to the 10% market share held by BIC, the innovator.[20]

Weapons in war and business are an important feature of combat. Weapons can convey an advantage but these advantages depend on a realistic understanding of the weapon's strengths and weaknesses, the use to which the weapon is put and the efforts made to preserve leadership in weapons development. The battlefield and market leverage of a weapon is frequently overestimated, particularly in terms of the reaction time of opponents. Throughout military history and in the market-place, armies and companies have continuously over-relied on a weapon to provide victory. While weapons can win battles, they invariably do not win wars. While the use of an Exocet missile by the Argentines in the Falkland Islands to sink the destroyer HMS Sheffield was a devastating success, it did not change the outcome of that war. The introduction of the Wankel rotary engine by Mazda and NSU in 1970 marked the first real advance on the standard automobile power plant, the otto-cycle piston engine, since the early 1900s. Despite the considerable benefits of small size, high power-to-weight ratio and low production costs the Wankel engines' early technical and fuel consumption problems prevented the revolutionary Wankel power plant from changing the face of the automobile engine market. Mazda's commitment to the Wankel engine was so great that it technically bankrupted Mazda in 1979 and NSU was fully absorbed into the Volkswagon-Audi Group in the mid-1970s and disappeared as an independent brand. New weapons seem to change both an army and a firm's concept of the territorial rights of competitors;

however, a weapon is only one component of an overall strategy rather than a strategy in itself. While military strategists have long understood the strategic weaknesses of a weapons–only strategy, business executives have still to recognize the limitations of a strategy based *totally* on a product, a production process, financial resources or a set of marketing techniques.

INTELLIGENCE

'We are following your advice, Vladimir Ilyich (Lenin), penetrating deeper and deeper into the enemy's plans'.

Feliks Dzherzhinsky

The use of intelligence as a military tool can be traced back to the Bible, and military commanders throughout history have made use of intelligence to provide details of any enemy's strength and positions as a means to assess their rivals' intentions and capabilities.

The Egyptians and the Assyrians, around 2000 BC, had effective intelligence systems. In the New Model Army of the Parliamentary forces during the English Civil War (1642—1651), a specific post of 'Scout-Master-General' was established to provide intelligence. Wellington thought that much of his success was due to his 'care in studying what was happening on the other side of the hill'.

Military Intelligence covers gathering and interpreting information.

GATHERING INFORMATION
Obtaining information differs markedly in peacetime and under combat conditions. During peace, intelligence is gathered by using overt and covert methods. Overt intelligence is obtained from a wide range of freely available information, from published sources, and through discussion and interview. Most embassies fulfil the role of collecting much of the overt economic, military and political information on their host countries. Covert intelligence, utilizing spies, has increased from the 1960s with developments in aerospace, electronics and optics technology, which provide the ability to monitor radio transmissions, break diplomatic and military codes using computers, and conduct continuous terrain surveillance using satellites.

Gathering intelligence during war moves the intelligence function primarily into the overt area. Reconnaissance patrols sent into the field to monitor an enemy's activities and to test and probe enemy defences are common intelligence gathering activities. The disastrous raid on Dieppe by the Canadians in 1942 was a reconaissance in force, to test the strength of the Atlantic Wall defences erected by the Germans to stop Allied landings in Northern France.

INTERPRETING INTELLIGENCE

Assessing data and drawing conclusions as to the implications of that information are crucial intelligence tasks. In the Cuban Missile Crisis (1962), US aerial reconnaissance indicated considerable construction in restricted areas in Cuba. The US correctly identified the build-up of Russian missile sites and by skilful use of photographic evidence at the United Nations and a strong naval blockade, forced the Soviet withdrawal of the missiles.

An effective intelligence organization plays a key role in military strategy. The Romans, widely regarded as a first-rate military power during their heyday, were frequently defeated as a result of a poor intelligence system and bad scouting. The latter stages of the American War of Independence (1775—1783) were characterized by the alienation of the population by the British, which deprived Cornwallis of the key ingredient to counter-insurgency warfare-intelligence.

To combat intelligence gathering by an enemy or potential opponent, two main weapons are used — counter-intelligence activities and deception. In the former case, the object is to locate and neutralize information gathering activities. Deception — supplying false information to the enemy — has been a major ploy throughout military history. The British used elaborate deceptions against the Germans in the 1939—1945 war. In preparation for D-Day in 1944 a phantom army commanded by Patton complete with dummy tanks and landing craft, supported by false radio traffic, was located opposite the Pas-de-Calais. Despite the D-Day landings in Normandy, the Germans believed that the main thrust of the invasion would come from Patton's phantom army and they kept several armoured divisions in reserve to repulse the expected landing. By accepting the deception, the Germans denied urgently needed reinforcement to their hard-pressed forces in Normandy. The use of deception has almost become institutionalized in military practice as a way to confuse the enemy and the Soviet intelligence organization, the KGB, maintains a section in the First Directorate, Department A, to spread disinformation.

The need for accurate information on competitors' plans and activities in business closely parallels military intelligence needs. Without information, a company is unable to form an idea of the competitor's strengths and weaknesses, or to anticipate a competitor's reactions to its own moves or to prevent a competitor interfering with its plans. Unlike military intelligence, business intelligence, for both ethical and business reasons, operates primarily in an overt manner gathering and interpreting available information rather than directly seeking proprietary information. Industrial espionage does exist as the charges brought against Mitsubishi and Hitachi in 1982 in the US for allegedly attempting to purchase IBM computer information suggest[21], and there are reputed to be at least three 'spy' schools, two in Japan and one in Switzerland, which turn out graduates in industrial espionage.[22]

Intelligence gathering activities in business are conducted along three broad lines — competitive intelligence, market intelligence and environment intelligence.

COMPETITIVE INTELLIGENCE

Competitive intelligence gathers and interprets information on actual and potential competitors' activities and identifies their strengths and weaknesses. The main source of competitive intelligence is published information available through electronic databases, the public and trade press, brokerage reports and annual company reports. In the technology–based industries, considerable competitive information can be obtained from scientific journals and patent applications. The increasing intervention of government in business activities, has produced a useful by–product in competitive information becoming available through specific reports analyzing companies and industries. A Monopolies Commission report on the industrial gases market in the UK in the early 1960s, which was dominated by British Oxygen (BOC), provided valuable information on the size and segments of the market and on BOC's production, distribution, costs and profits which a new competitor, Air Products, successfully used to enter the market.

In the USA, the Freedom of Information Act of 1966 and its potent 1974 amendment has created a cottage industry of information providers in Washington, supplying competitive information to companies. Companies also obtain information on competitor's activities through scientific and trade conferences by taking plant tours and aerial photographs, debriefing design consultants, milking potential employees, conducting false interviews, luring people away from competitors, through interviews with customers and suppliers and even buying competitors' rubbish.[23]

IBM so dominates the computer industry that its plans affect the calculations of countless other firms. Few companies are as secretive as IBM about their future activities and an industry of 'watchers' has sprung up questioning customers, combing technical literature and studying corporate statements in an attempt to identify IBM's intentions. Input, one of the 'watchers', was able to correctly predict IBM's re-entry into the computer servicing market after a ten year absence. IBM was transferring high level software and marketing staff to a secret project in Florida which Input discovered from IBM staff who did not want to relocate, and confirmed by examining local hiring information.[24] Reverse engineering is a common intelligence weapon in industries with rapid technological change. Business machine, camera, car, computer, consumer electronics, power-tool and watch companies routinely strip down rival products to identify competitive cost, design features, performance characteristics and production methods. Mosaid, for example, has built a business specializing in reverse engineering of semiconductor chips to find out how they work and supplies the information as a paid service to semiconductor manufacturers.[25]

The increasing number of airlines and passenger seats available in the USA following airline de-regulation in 1978, led to major price wars, and competitive intelligence became a key factor in managing fares to maximize revenues under intense competition. Delta Airlines' 147-strong tariff department makes extensive use of computers to track and analyze the 5,000 or so daily airline industry price changes registered by Air Tariff Publishing. By analyzing fare changes Delta can identify major changes in competitors' monopoly routes which can signify system-wide price changes and gauge the level of competition by the amount of price adjustments made by other airlines. Delta reinforces its competitive intelligence with telephone calls to competitors, posing as prospective clients, and input from its field office and reservations staff, who alert Delta to price changes (picked up in local newspapers) made by competing airlines, who delay disclosure through Air Tariff Publishing in an attempt to get a few days competitive advantage. Delta's intelligence system enables the airline to regulate discount fare seats to maximize revenue, and to help decide whether to refer tour group discount requests to another airline to help fill that competitor's plane with low fare passengers and thereby drive other passengers into the full fare seats available on Delta. The system also forecasts how many seats Delta should hold for last minute full fare business passengers in lucrative markets such as New York, where more than half the passengers book seats less than 72 hours before departure. Delta's competitive intelligence system is credited with making a major contribution to profits (without putting more planes in the air, opening up new routes or launching extensive discount promotions) by carefully matching, rather than leading, the fare discount wars in the US airline industry.[26]

MARKET INTELLIGENCE

Market intelligence focuses on monitoring trends in the market to identify future problems and opportunities, and provides a company with the information necessary to manœuvre in advance of the change in the market.

In the mid-1970s Pittston Coal, the seventh largest US coal producer, lost sales in its metallurgical-grade coal (used in coke for steel making) as a result of steel industry overcapacity and the downturn in world steel markets. Pittston identified a significant opportunity in the 'compliance' market for their low-sulphur metallurgic coal for electric utilities which could burn Pittston's coal with low pollution, eliminating the need to install expensive flue scrubber systems.[27]

Ford recognized, through the rapid growth in sales of GM's

Monza conversion of the Corvair and imported European sports cars, that a major US market was evolving for sporty cars as part of the 1960s orientation towards youth. Ford rapidly developed and introduced the Mustang, in 1964, to fill the gap in its product line to meet new consumer needs. By 1966 over 1 million Mustangs had been sold, over 50% to people who had not previously owned a Ford. The Mustang, tailor-made to fit an emerging market need, was one of the major innovative car products of the 1960s.

A surge occured in the commuter aircraft market in the US following airline de-regulation in 1978. A number of low-density routes were abandoned by the larger carriers when the rising costs of fuel made continued service uneconomical, even with smaller jets. This opened up the market for rugged commuter turbo-prop aircraft which could fly the routes profitably. A number of foreign manufacturers anticipated that as soon as the OPEC prices began moving up, the DC9, a 100-seat jet used by regional airlines on short stages would become uneconomic. By concentrating single-mindedly on business in hand, the US commuter aircraft manu-facturers failed to see the double impact of rising fuel costs and de-regulation. By expecting a gradual expansion of commuter services and by eschewing passenger appeal with their existing aircraft, Cessna and Piper missed out on an entire generation of aircraft orders. The remaining US manufacturer, Beech, concentrated production on an unpressurized 15-seat commuter aircraft which did not meet the need for a 15- to 50-seat commuter aircraft — the most in demand. The larger aircraft of De Havilland Canada, Embraer and Short filled a number of niches in the US commuter aircraft market while the domestic companies were trying to establish just what constituted the market.[28]

ENVIRONMENTAL INTELLIGENCE
This intelligence is directed at identifying trends in the environment such as social, political, economic and technological change which may impact the business. The use of environmental intelligence by companies has increased in response to both the disequilibrium created by the OPEC price increases and sociological changes.

Environmental intelligence can provide valuable early warning signals for business. The growth in the Right-to-Life movement and the Hyde Amendment to the US Health, Education and Welfare Departments' 1977 budget which placed sharp limits on the use of federal funds for abortions for Medicaid clients signalled a possible threat to the existence of abortion clinics which had emerged in the US during the early 1970s. By identifying this threat and the possibility that this movement would succeed in barring legal abortions, many of the clinics began to diversify into the out-patient medical services market by offering a variety of services such as simple surgery, sex counselling, fertility help, birth control, prenatal care and a host of other reproductive medical services for both men and women. Inadvertently, the abortion clinics had begun a major pioneering role in sex-related out-patient services from a limited service base as a result of anticipating possible social and political pressures on their original business.[29]

Liggett & Myers, the smallest US cigarette manufacturer, correctly identified a trend towards cost containment in the brand-dominated US cigarette market, in response to the economic recession, inflation and unemployment which was heightened by the rising local, state and federal excise taxes on cigarettes. L&M launched generic cigarettes into the market in 1980 to meet the anticipated demand for low priced alternatives to branded cigarettes and by 1983 was producing 96% of the $590 million new market for generic cigarettes. L&M's move was both a tactical success in opening up a new market segment as well as a strategic success bringing in cash to a faltering company. By 1983 generics accounted for around 60% of L&M's sales of $562 million and helped to increase pre-tax profits to $60 million reversing a 30 year decline in the company's fortunes.[30]

In contrast, the baby-food manufacturers in Europe failed to anticipate the full severity of declining birth rates and changing medical opinion which persuaded more and more women to breast-feed babies. The European market for baby-foods by 1980 had fallen by about 5% in real terms from 1976 and in some countries the percentage of women breast-feeding their babies had doubled during the 1970s. Exports to the developing countries with their high birth rates had also grown very slowly due to criticism over promotional campaigns which had not properly educated mothers on the use of milk products as a subsitute for breast-feeding. By failing to spot these trends at an early stage, the market was plunged into confusion. Gerber, for example, decided to withdraw from most markets, the leading British firm Cow & Gate sought a buyer, and internecine warfare occured as firms sought to maintain volume by moving aggressively into each other's domestic markets. Other companies attempted to extend the age range of their products to pre-school children which forced them into direct competition with the cereal giants General Foods and Kellogg.[31]

Similarly, Mary Kay Cosmetics failed to appreciate social and economic trends which severely impacted its direct sales organization in the US in 1983. Both recruitment and direct sales volume are based on networks of relationships which began to crumble as social changes such as divorce, relocation and new life-styles became pronounced. This, coupled with the improvement in the US economy, which prompted more women to avoid part-time sales work and enabled increasing numbers of women to shop for more expensive cosmetics, caused Mary Kay's recruitment program to maintain a 200,000 person sales force and its direct sales volume to falter.[32]

Intelligence plays a vital role in military and business combat — as Napoleon remarked 'to be defeated is pardonable: to be surprised, Never!'

While military intelligence has become indispensable to combat success, business intelligence has yet to reach similar levels of acceptance. Most business intelligence is provided by the marketing function, but the full value of intelligence is lost unless there is a system of collecting and interpreting information across functions. Few companies, for example, have gone as far as Nestlé in appointing a senior executive to manage internal and external information. As the fight for market share increases, the ability to gather and interpret information more efficiently and effectively than competitors becomes a key weapon for survival. Gillette carefully tracked BIC's progress with disposable razors in Europe and Canada in the mid-1970s and was able to mount a formidable and successful counter-attack with its own disposable razor when BIC entered the US market in 1976. In contrast ITEL, a computer leasing company, failed to identify IBM's development of a new line of computers superior to the equipment ITEL owned and leased out. When IBM introduced its new line in 1979 ITEL's computer leasing business collapsed as customers moved away from ITEL's obsolete equipment. ITEL's profits evaporated from $47 million in 1978 into a loss of $430 million in 1979.[33] The maxim 'To be forewarned is to be forearmed' is equally relevant to business as it is to war.

ORGANIZATION AND LEADERSHIP

`It is very easy for ignorant people to think that success in war may be gained by the use of some wonderful invention rather than by hard fighting and superior leadership`.

General George S. Patton

The way in which armies are organized and prepared and how they are led in battle have long been identified as key elements for combat success.

Although primitive combat was based on individual fighting or massed hordes, organized armies had become the rule as early as 4000 BC. These armed organizations had become relatively sophisticated as early as 2900 BC, when the Sumerians used a Citizen Phalanx. The Byzantine Horse-army, the Carthaginian Navy, the Doric Phalanx and the Roman Legion were vastly superior organizational concepts to that which had gone before and were scarcely matched until the middle of the seventeenth century. Until the emergence of Gustavus Adolphus of Sweden in 1621, armies had degenerated from the highly professional Roman armies into undisciplined, amateurish, affairs led by incompetent noblemen. Gustavus Adolphus created one of the first 'modern' standing armies by training, paying, disciplining and uniforming his troops to instil professional pride. This, allied to new tactics emphasizing mobility and firepower, gave Gustavus Adolphus many of his victories in the Thirty Years War (1618—1648). Around the same time, Oliver Cromwell produced the first really professional army in England — the 'New Model Army'. While both Frederick the Great (1713—1786) and Napoleon (1769—1821) perfected inherited armies, one of the most lasting marks on military organization was made by a succession of Prussians in the nineteenth century — von Scharnhorst, von Moltke and von Schlieffen, who developed and perfected the professional staff system which centralized command. It was not until the early twentieth century that Britain and France emulated a regular staff system with the efficiency and quality of the Prussian model. The size of armed forces grew as agrarian, economic and population resources increased, and the scale of battle became larger as it was recognized that superior numbers were relevant to the outcome of battle. This in turn required greater organizational and administrative skills to mass, manœuvre and provision large numbers of troops. The increase in offensive and defensive weapons technology in the twentieth century brought additional problems in that sophisticated support elements were required to operate and maintain complex weaponry and to support mechanized forces. Frequently the support elements began to outnumber the troops used in battle. In Vietnam the US had some 7 non-combatants in the rear supporting every combatant at the front. However there are exceptions. The Israeli Self Defence Force, one of the most successful modern fighting units, has a very high ratio of combatants to non-combatants despite its emphasis on sophisticated weaponry.

Professionalism is a key feature of all successful military institutions. While airforces and navies have always exhibited a high degree of professionalism, due to their dependence on complex weaponry, the shift in the officer corps in armies from amateurism to professionalism took centuries. The development of the first truly professional approach to war by the Prussians in the nineteenth century showed conclusively in the Franco-Prussian War (1870—1871), that a nation taking the profession of arms seriously could completely outmatch a country, France, using a nation-in-arms approach to warfare. The allied officer corps in the First World War, where combat experience was largely derived from colonial wars, were poorly prepared to face the German war machine with its Prussian legacy of professionalism, or to rapidly adapt to the changing nature of battle. The amateur allied officer corps did not have the intellectual capacity to be able to break out of the prison of their colonial experience to counter the dedicated professionalism of the German army or the transformation of war to automatic weapons, barbed wire, trench warfare, and high explosives which had been signalled by the Russo-Japanese conflict a decade earlier. Bravery, to compensate for the lack of professional ability, caused large combat losses. For example, on the second day of the Battle of Loos (1915) the British blindly attacked a well fortified position with 10,000 men. The British took over 80% losses while the Germans managed to retain the position with ease and suffered no casualties. The lessons of the First World War changed the Allied approach to professionalism. Staffing became based on recruitment of volunteers rather than conscripted forces and a radical re-organization, emphasizing high levels of education and training, and better compensation with promotion linked to intellectual ability, was initiated to broaden the range of skills of officers, to develop mental, moral, and physical qualities, and to attract and retain the highest calibre of individual. Continuous education became a main feature of the professional approach to prepare officers for greater levels of responsibility and to extend experience as a rational approach to career development, promotion, and compensation.

Leadership of armed forces has developed along similar lines to organization. Early conflict was controlled in a highly personal fashion where senior officers almost always led combat units and success depended entirely on the skills and abilities of one individual. Frequently, the death or disablement of a commander led to the defeat or withdrawal of his army. Even as late as the nineteenth century it was not uncommon for senior commanders to be involved in close action. Marlborough, Napoleon and Wellington were all, at one time or another in the later stages in their careers, almost killed in combat and both Gustavus Adolphus and Charles XII of Sweden died on the battlefield. During the First World War with the continuous front, commanders tended to direct combat from the rear. However, the return to fluid warfare in the Second World War (since it was recognized that battles are won or lost on the tactical level), has required that senior commanders get close to combat. The success of 'fighting' generals such as Montgomery, Patton and Rommel, in the Second World War and Sharon in the various Israeli Wars, was largely due to their personal involvement in directing combat at the front. While the qualities for good generalship have been debated over the centuries, no ideal has emerged since different types of combat require different types of skills. Although a great many traits have been suggested for good generalship, the most important is the capability to manage people well under combat conditions. However, even this quality is open to wide interpretation. Autocratic commanders, such as Frederick the Great, Wellington and Patton, not noted as humanitarians with the welfare of their troops uppermost in their minds, performed equally as well in combat as their more democratic welfare-orientated opposites, Marlborough, Bradley and Montgomery.

Management techniques began to make an impact on the military in the 20th century when it was recognized that large-scale logistic needs, complex technology, and the cost of sophisticated weapons systems demanded centralized control of deployment, transportation, procurement, and training. Following the successful managerial experience of the First World War, where the US moved two million men and seven and a half million tons of material to Europe in less than nineteen months, and of the Normandy Invasion in the Second World War (1944), where the Allies in the first forty-eight hours, organized three million men, 12,000 aircraft and 4,600 vessels to support the landing of 150,000 troops and 1,500 tanks, management technique began to dominate US military thinking. Since armed forces are mirrors of their own societies, it was probably inevitable that the important role of business in the US economy, where a premium was placed on management techniques, would have a major influence on the US military establishment. In the Robert McNamara era of the 1960s, with a Defence Secretary direct from Ford Motor Company, the application of management techniques to military situations became a routine procedure throughout the US armed forces as a support to, and later even as a substitute for, leadership. The emphasis on technical expertise in the US Navy, for example, ensured that most nuclear submarine captains were nuclear engineers who had risen to command posts never having fired a shot in anger in any type of naval warfare. The overemphasis on management and the growing subordination of leadership to management resulted in the de-personalization of officers and troops which, together with short tours of duty and frequent rotation, broke down the trust between officers and men and reduced a unit's resistance to combat stress. Officers began to concentrate on careers which were seen as more important than the units with the effect that the units began to lose sight of themselves as recognizable entities. In the early 1980s, the US military began to revert back to the regimental system in the army and reduce crew rotation in the air force and also increased the duty tours to improve group combat cohesion, through the re-emphasis of leadership. The UK, on the other hand, with less emphasis on business technique and a greater regimental tradition avoided, for the most, these pitfalls. The British performance in the Falklands War, for example, proved that when 'the chips were down' loyalty to the group rather than an abstract loyalty to a country became a significant factor in combat success.

As in military combat, considerable attention has been focused in business on both organization and leadership and there are close parallels. Market combat in small-scale companies is largely based on individualized fighting in the market by the entrepreneur and the organization, which, although centralized, tends to be rudimentary and frequently limited to servicing the firm's minimal financial, production and customer obligations. As companies grow, their financial, productive and human resources increase; and the scale of market conflict grows as firms increase their product and service offerings to reach more customers and enter new markets, and as they expand internationally. This in turn requires greater organizational and administrative skills to mass, manœuvre and supply large numbers of employees. As the scale of business operations increases and the techniques and technology of business become more complex the number and authority of staff groups increases. This has the general effect that more people become involved in administration than in the most important combat roles at the front — designing, manufacturing, selling and servicing products.

There are notable exceptions. Mars, a $5 billion privately-owned confectionary and pet-food company, has less than 40 people at their headquarters in the US and makes almost three times the industry's return on investment, while the Grand Metropolitan conglomerate, one of the most successful UK companies, has less than 25 people at their head office.

Few organizational concepts in business are truly new and most have been unconsciously borrowed from the military. DuPont and General Motors developed the divisional organizational structure in the mid-1930s which had its origins one hundred and thirty years before in Carnots' divisionalization of the French Army in 1794. Similarly, the Strategic Business Unit (SBU) concept of a standalone business profit centre, pioneered by General Electric in the US in the early 1970s, has its parallel one hundred and seventy years before in 1800 in Napoleon's Corps D'Armée concept of a self-contained miniature army with its own staff which could fight alone and was able to march semi-independently from the rest of the Grande Armée. One organizational concept present only in business is the matrix structure which was developed to handle complex organizational problems posed by multi-product companies operating multi-nationally with multi-functional requirements. However, matrix structures do not seem to be able to manage complex sets of interfaces because of the diffusion of control and responsibility. Xerox, for example, almost strangled itself with a matrix structure. The heads of production, planning, design and service were based in Rochester, New York, and each reported to separate corporate executives in Connecticut. Each group passed products through its own hierarchy, with endless debates over features and design trade-offs, and then on to headquarters, with the result that no one person or group had responsibility for ensuring that products moved quickly from conception to the market-place.[34] The reason that the military does not use matrix type structures is that battles are not won by diffusing control and responsibility — a point which companies locked in market conflict would be wise to follow. While it has been recognized in business that structure follows strategy with the implication that companies should structure themselves to pursue a particular type of strategy, few firms adopt this combat-orientated organizational concept. Unlike armies few companies are truly structured for market combat — they are organized to administer — and in consequence are less able to fight successfully in the market.

There are startling similarities in the effects of the strategic style of organizations in war and business. Allied strategic style in both world wars was conditioned by the fact that officer education was aimed at the management of men and the provision of material for combat while German officers were taught almost exclusively how to lead troops and manœuvre their combat resources. Western business education focuses firmly on the management of human and physical resources and functions, while the Japanese, with few formal business schools, are taught, through their general in-company experience-related business education, how to employ the company's resources. In allied military and western business education the actual employment of force appears to be secondary to the marshalling of muscle. In both world wars Germany had greatly inferior resources to those of its enemies yet the German army outperformed its enemies to a notable degree before being defeated by this lack of resources and not by its lack of combat skills. In similar vein the leading Japanese companies in western markets were once greatly inferior in assets to their resource-rich western competitors; however, they have outperformed their western counterparts in industries as diverse as cars, cameras, consumer electronics, motorcycles, ships, steel and zip fasteners to a remarkable degree. Unlike the German army, few Japanese companies have expanded beyond their organizational capabilities and resources, and have not been defeated by their lack of resources. Victory on the battlefield and in the market–place achieved through brute force or the sheer quantity of resources tends to subsume issues of strategy, and yet strategic organizational style is a key factor in the quality of combat skills and their effective use in both war and business.

Business has moved much more slowly towards professionalism than the military, and in most companies the development of a truly professional approach to organizing and conducting battles for market share is at an early stage. In business education, the emphasis is on one pre–employment, long, concentrated, dose of professional training — for example, the MBA, accountancy and legal qualifications — after which the executive is regarded as qualified even though he is a novice. The average executive probably spends a lot less than 8% of his 40—45 year working life in job related skills improvement programmes, as compared with more than 20% by his military counterpart. Future promotion in business is rarely linked to qualifications from continuous formal education programmes, with the effect that the executive is not encouraged to develop a broadly–based skills package. Inevitably, the executive is poorly prepared to face the changing nature of markets brought about by radical technological, economic, social, and competitive change. The feudal nature of promotion and compensation systems, used by many companies and depending largely on patronage, places the executive in a position where he has little choice but to concentrate on his career, which is seen as more important than the company. Putting career self–interest ahead of the company, fosters intense internal competition which can wreck a company's cohesion. Promotion and reward systems based on financial performance measurements are subjective, since they are more applicable to some than others, suffer from discontinuity as performance fluctuates, and above all are mercenary, since they subject an executive to progression and reward based on a 'body count' of sales and profits.

A further complication is that most western companies have great difficulty in successfully executing strategic manœuvres due to reward systems which link compensation and promotion to short term tactical performance which, while helping to win battles in the market, can often lose competitive wars in the mid– to long–term. In contrast Japanese companies with reward systems linking compensation and promotion largely to tenure and seniority have generally been more successful in executing long-term strategies. For example, in the US and European car markets Nissan and Toyota took over a decade to secure a viable share of the market which required a long term investment in sales and service facilities.

By treating executives as mercenaries rather than professionals, companies run the risk that executives will act like mercenaries, and switch employment to competitors offering a better career and compensation package. Mercenary treatment, job rotation, and short tenures weaken the executive leadership role which in turn reduce the company's resistance to the stresses of market conflict. The current performance problems of many companies have been largely attributed to the effects of the recession, when arguably companies would have been better placed to overcome the impact of the recession if they had placed a greater premium in the past on executive professionalism.

The Sainsbury — Tesco battle in the UK grocery market is an excellent example of the use of professionalism to produce higher levels of performance than the market leader. Sainsbury, using a strategy emphasizing high quality at competitive prices in well-appointed outlets and a highly professional approach to its business, managed to significantly reduce the commanding sales level of its rival, Tesco, in the highly competitive UK grocery market from almost 20% in 1979 to less than 4% in 1983. Tesco's style of entrepreneurial decentralized control with local store purchasing and direct suppliers' delivery to individual stores, overmanning and small store sizes was extremely vulnerable to Sainsbury's professional approach. Sainsbury's focus on centralized control, purchasing and distribution in large outlets, enabled them to emphasize efficiency and significantly reduce costs. While Tesco had almost 5 million square feet of retail space in 403 stores; Sainsbury, with 3.9 million square feet in 242 stores, was able to achieve about 15.5% of the UK packaged grocery market — a two percentage point gap over Tesco — and by 1983 Sainsbury's profit margins, at 4.4%, were almost twice that of Tesco's.

In contrast, in many high technology industries where the objective is to bring new products to the market to meet continuous technological change, companies are often run by engineers and scientists and professional management plays a secondary role in favour of innovation and production. Both Hewlett-Packard (HP) and Digital Equipment (DEC) were slow to develop and sell personal computers. In HP and DEC several autonomous units developed their own personal computers with the result that salesmen from the same company got in each other's way and customers often found that the new computers were not compatible with the companies' other products. Both companies were re-organized in 1983—1984 to make marketing as important as innovating and producing and to provide a more professional approach to their businesses.[35] In almost all biotechnology companies scientists straight from academia, with no prior business experience, dominate management. The declining share values and lack of success in raising adequate additional capital to fund long-term research suggests that the financial community places a low level of credibility on the professionalism of many of these companies and on their ability to survive.

There are leadership elements in business analogous to those of the military. Small-scale companies tend to be controlled in a highly personal fashion and survival depends on the skills and abilities of one person — Sir Clive Sinclair of Sinclair Research in the UK is a prime example.[36] The death or departure of the key individual from the firm frequently signals the end of that firm's combat capability. As firms become larger and more complex, management tends to direct combat from the rear with the result that distance distorts the reality of combat and morale suffers. However, some companies firmly believe in executives directing combat at the front-line. At IBM and Digital Equipment, top management spend at least 30 days a year conferring with key customers, and no manager at IBM holds a staff job for more than three years since it is believed that management staff are out of the mainstream because they do not meet customers regularly.[37] Digital Equipment's decision in 1982 to decentralize in Europe from its Geneva headquarters was due in part to the need to base the marketing organizations close to the production facilities and to the customers. In the highly competitive computer industry both IBM and Digital Equipment follow the maxim that battles are won or lost at the tactical level. The success of Thomas Watson of IBM, a 'fighting' executive, was largely due to his personal involvement in directing combat in the field. Other highly successful companies such as Hewlett–Packard, Marks & Spencer and Pepsi–Cola have a highly visible management which communicates effectively by using the technique of managing by walking around.

Leadership qualities in management, as in the military, are the subject of continued debate; however, the man–management aspect prevails as the most dominant trait and similarly, autocrats vie with democrats in terms of success. Harold Geneen of ITT, Charles Revson of Revlon, Edwin Land of Polaroid, Sir John Davis of Rank–Xerox were highly successful as autocrats while Lord Sieff of Marks & Spencer, Sir Peter Masefield at British European Airways, and George Rosenkranz at Syntex were equally successful as democratic managers, under market combat conditions. Over-organization and bad management can be as fatal to armies as they can to companies. The model army left by Frederick the Great had become an over–administered nightmare by the early 1800s and suffered decisive defeats by Napoleon at Auerstadt and Jena (1806), which annihilated the Prussian army. Over–centralized command by remote control was one of the key ingredients of the US 1st Armoured Division's defeat by the Afrika Korps in 1943 at Kasserine Pass. Similarly, in the early 1980s General Electric of the US had become a centralized bureaucracy and was consistently beaten on costs by Emerson Electric, a much smaller competitor, which manufactured its products in plants with fewer than 600 employees.[38] The succession of failures against the Confederate Forces in the 1861—1864 period resulted in five changes in command in the Union Army and finally Ulysses S. Grant's appointment provided the leadership necessary to win the American Civil War. Henry Ford's autocratic management style which prevented his managers from managing, led to a number of bad managerial decisions, one of which (the long response time to General Motors who introduced the idea of an annual change in body styling in 1923) lost Ford the leadership of the US automobile market from which Ford has never recovered.

The impact of US management techniques on the business world has had a major influence on the way in which companies are operated and in how they have developed since the turn of the century. However, the emphasis on technique has led many companies into the trap of overmanagement and the confusion of management with leadership. Management (knowing what to do) and leadership (getting it done) are not the same thing. The greater the distance from the sharp end of competitive conflict the more need there is for management and, conversely, the closer to the action in the market the greater need there is for leadership. While both traits are highly important, neither management nor leadership are mutually exclusive components of success. Business courses, however, are full of programmes of management technique, but there are remarkably few training courses designed to develop leadership skills. The concentration on management technique to the detriment of leadership has had a direct effect on the ability of companies to carry through strategic manœuvres at the tactical level in the market. Since battles for market share are won in the market-place and not in the executive command bunker, the lack of emphasis on leadership may partially explain poor corporate performance. The heavy emphasis on management technique has helped create a corps of consumate business managers rewarded for their administrative skills rather than build a cadre of resourceful leaders who have been rewarded for their combat prowess fighting competition in the market.

The pattern of evolution and operation of armies and companies are strikingly similar since both are tribal societies. Both forms of endeavour have hierarchical structures of organization and patterns of behaviour including value systems, customs and attitudes which have been institutionalized by example, passed on to succeeding generations and hardened by success into custom.[39] In the final analysis, effective organization and leadership are essential elements for success to any army or firm. However, they can also be the greatest enemy of each institution if they are allowed to become the end rather than the means to an end and prevent the organization from fulfilling its true mission — that of winning the battle. Companies, like armies, get what they ask for, which in turn is a reflection of what they are. Without a dedication to professionalism in terms of attracting, training, developing, motivating and retaining executives, companies are amateurish organizations, and, however gifted, will ultimately fail against more professional adversaries. The fact that companies from a diverse set of industries, such as Boeing, BMW, Matsushita, IBM, Marks & Spencer, Mars, Merck & Co., Procter & Gamble, Kodak, Schlumberger and YKK, dominate their markets so entirely is due to their high level of professionalism, which has consistently defeated challenges from more innovative but much more amateurish competitors.

COMMUNICATION

'Communications dominate war; broadly considered they are the most important single element in strategy, political or military'.

Admiral Alfred Mahan.

Accurate and timely communication has proved essential in military combat throughout history as it provides commanders with the ability to evaluate changing conditions and to make the necessary responses to meet new situations. Good communication is essential to close teamwork amongst both units and allies. Marlborough and Eugene at Blenheim (1704) exhibited a far greater degree of co-operation through good communication than their opponents Tallard, Marsin and the Elector of Bavaria who lost the battle through their lack of co-operation and communication.

The growth in the size of battles and the geographic dispersion of forces placed an increasing emphasis on the need for good communication. Until the electric telegraph in the 1850s, military communications were transmitted by a variety of methods including runners, horse-mounted couriers, pigeons, dogs and later the heliograph and balloons. The availability of both the electric telegraph and the railway system revolutionized co-ordinated large-scale military movements and proved to be decisive in both the American Civil War (1861—1865) and the Franco-Prussian War (1870—1871). However, until the introduction of the wireless during the First World War (1914–1918), armies were completely reliant on line communication. In the 1970s electronic communication, particularly in the form of satellites, and airborne command posts again revolutionized military combat since they not only removed the reliance on line communications but also largely overcame the geographic co-ordination problems associated with military campaigns in far flung areas of the world. The use by the British of US satellites for communication in the Falklands War (1982) some 8,000 miles from Britain, provided the British with a communication and therefore a co-ordination edge over the Argentines.

Communications have proved to be an indispensable aid to successful business combat enabling operating units to quickly respond to changing conditions. Although IBM is rarely at the forefront of new computer technology it has the ability through its highly developed communications to rapidly co-ordinate the development of complex new products which are better designed, marketed and serviced than its competitors. IBM, for example, entered the personal computer market five years after Apple had created the market and pioneered the technology. Within two years IBM had secured leadership of the personal computer market from Apple through its ability to co-ordinate a superior response to competition. In contrast, a bizarre lack of co-ordination between autonomous operating divisions led to a situation where General Motors actually outmanœuvred itself. In the late 1960s Pontiac was the third largest selling car manufacturer in the US focusing on sporty youthful cars with a distinctive high-powered 'muscle' image. The change of customer emphasis in the late 1970s and 1980s to safer, low pollution and more economical cars clashed with Pontiac's macho image. The other GM divisions independently began to pressure Pontiac. Chevrolet increased prices to cover costs and focused on fuel efficiency. Buick and Oldsmobile reduced prices to remain competitive and focused on styling and all three divisions developed ranges of cars. Pontiac was caught without large cars and with an image inconsistent with the volume market and where the major differences between GM's cars was the name-plate and trim. Customers were not prepared to pay the $300 or so price differential for a Pontiac since there was no perceived product value over Chevrolet, while Buick and Oldsmobile offered more opulent cars. By 1982 Pontiac ranked fifth in sales of US cars due to the lack of co-ordination between GM's divisions.[40]

Communications between operating units in business has largely followed the military and similar methods of communication have been adopted, primarily line communication by telephone, telex and telegraph. Commercial satellite communication in the 1970s has added a new dimension to business combat, particularly for the multi-country company to co-ordinate campaigns over large geographic distances. Merck, for example, was using multi-country symposia conducted via satellite links between the US and Europe as early as 1978 to introduce physicians to new products. While firms have not yet been able to emulate direct communication down to the platoon level with, for example, sales forces, the availability of personal computers, electronic mail, cellular mobile radio-phones and low cost CB radios may provide companies with the same degree of communication quality and flexibility enjoyed by their military counterparts.

The growth in size of the firm and the fact that the market–place has become international rather than national, with the effect that competitive aggression is now a global reality, forces a company to view communication as an essential combat support element. While good communications are essential on the battlefield and in the market–place, both armies and companies do not always listen to the message — with equally disastrous consequences. Admiral Sir John Fisher in 1903, and the then recently formed Imperial General Staff in 1906 and again in 1911, reviewed the Dardanelles in terms of forcing a passage and disembarking armies on the Gallipoli peninsula and came to the conclusion that it would be too hazardous. These observations were ignored by politicians and a disastrous campaign was waged in 1915 with the inevitable outcome. Similarly, for many years, dealer and customer complaints flowed into BL concerning poor quality of the Jaguar car. Belatedly, Jaguar cured the problems in late 1981 but was then forced into a costly relaunch of the Marque and of luring customers away from BMW and Mercedes where they had flocked in preference to the poor quality Jaguar XJ-6 and XJ-12 models.

LOGISTICS

'Without supplies no army is brave'.

Frederick the Great.

Provisioning and supplying a combat unit is indispensable to its ability to fight. Without an adequate supply of food, clothing, shelter, fuel and ammunition, any armed force will come to a grinding halt.

Through to the seventeenth century, provisioning was limited largely to the amount that could be carried by individual combatants and in convoys of wagons. Resupply, a rather fragile endeavour, was supplemented by foraging at the expense of local populations. While foraging has become an institutionalized occupation of armies it was realized that the amount of supplies available in the immediate theatre of operations could be limited and populations alienated, and during the seveneenth century, pre-stocked depots began to be used with supplies being convoyed to the battle area.

Until the development of railway systems, armies were logistically restricted in their operational range and by the time required to prepare for combat. Superior logistics in the American Civil War (1861—1865) and the Franco-Prussian War (1870—1871) based on the extensive use of railways, were decisive to the Union and Prussian victories. The fact that the outnumbered Confederate forces were able to remain in the field for four years was largely due to General Josiah Gorgas, Chief of Ordnance, who created a munitions industry from scratch, and kept the Confederates supplied with locally produced material or by blockade running. The Israelis successfully built a 'cottage' armament and munitions industry to supply their forces in the first Arab-Israeli War (1948). Through a sustained policy of self-sufficiency, Israel developed a high technology armaments industry which by the mid-1970s had become a major factor in the international arms trade. In contrast, the once invincible Grande Armée of Napoleon suffered notable defeats in the Peninsular War (1807—1814) and in Russia (1812), by neglecting its logistical support which progressively reduced the army's ability to fight sustained actions. By destroying or disrupting an enemy's logistical system an aggressor can isolate and contract conflict. Submarine warfare in both world wars almost brought the British to a halt until effective counter-measures in the form of convoys, long-range patrol aircraft and, from the 1930s, Sonar, were adopted.

Logistical support is as important to a company as it is to an army. Without an adequate supply of raw materials, production capability, distribution and product support companies cannot compete effectively in the market.

The equity position taken by a number of chemical and pharmaceutical companies in biotechnology companies was due to the potential of genetic engineering to produce products in short supply from traditional sources, and thereby ensure a dependable supply of low cost raw materials. Burroughs never recovered from production problems with its computer line in the 1970s which diverted sales to other manufacturers.[41] Vickers Aircraft's limited production line for the highly successful turbine-powered Viscount airliner delayed deliveries in the late 1950s with the result that General Dynamics' obsolescent piston-engined Convair 440 picked up a number of additional orders notably from SAS and Swissair at the Viscount's expense.

Adequate distribution of the final product or service is an essential feature of market–place combat. Heineken's premier position in the US imported beer market is largely due to its excellent national distribution system which leads to fast turnover, ensuring fresh beer, and thereby reinforcing Heineken's quality image.[42] In contrast Apple disenchanted its only distribution channel, independent retailers, with the poor performance of the initial supplies of the Apple III computer in the US and largely ignored retailers' complaints. Facing increased competition, notably from IBM which was new to the market, Apple belatedly embarked on a major campaign to court its retailers in late 1982.[43]

Some businesses owe their life–blood to logistics. American Hospital Supply (AHSC) built a $3 billion business by developing a state–of–the–art computer–based manufacturing and distribution network that enabled the company to beat its competitors and become the largest distributor of hospital supplies in the United States. Through its innovative distribution strategy in a business with low margins, a 200,000 item product line, considerable warehousing and delivery services, and little product differentiation, AHSC climbed from sixth to first place with a 20% share of a highly fragmented market and grew to three times the size of its nearest competitor within a decade.[44] To overcome the complex distribution system in Japan a number of western companies have used unconventional distribution strategies which have been highly successful. Eversharp distributes its Schick razors and blades through a cutlery wholesaler; Wella designed its shampoos as beauty aids and distributed them through drugstores and beauty parlours rather than supermarkets; and McDonalds avoids its US strategy of putting its fast food outlets in the suburbs and concentrates on the teeming city centres.[45]

Product support is also an essential logistical element in the market–place. The ability to supply sales forces with both mobility and with sufficient supplies for sales promotion, and customers with adequate after–sales service, is indispensable in market combat. IBM, for example, has an enviable reputation for its highly trained, well supplied and professional sales and service force. In the UK, Hoover built a strong position in the durable electrical goods market with an army of service engineers during the 1950s, and Caterpillar promises a forty-eight hour guaranteed parts service anywhere in the world and if it cannot meet the promise the customer gets the part free.

Despite the fact that logistics are of key importance in military and business combat, logistics have been ignored by ninety-nine military historians out of a hundred and there are remarkably few references in the business press to logistics. The Confederate General Nathan Forrest suggested that combat success was 'to get there first with the most men', but without an effective logistical system armies and companies cannot move, let alone fight.

SUMMARY

The support elements are *the* key resources of companies and armies since no strategy — deterrent, offence, defence or alliance — can be successfully executed in business or in war without effective support. Support elements, the basic functions and operating skills, are the core of a company's or an army's strength. Both derive their relative combat positions from the way in which executives and generals strike a balance between the relative strengths of each of the support elements and the way in which this balance is fine-tuned to meet the demands of the market-place or battlefield.

Companies fail in the market-place because:

1. Few strategic manoeuvres integrate more than one or two of the core support elements resulting in an iceberg strategy which leaves the bulk of the firm's skills submerged and never brought to bear on competition.

2. Companies try to 'fit' the support elements to a strategy rather than designing the manoeuvre to fit the strengths of the company's core skills and resources.

Companies fight battles in the market with technological, production, financial and marketing weapons; they need information on the enemy (competition), the battlefield (market) and the terrain (environment); organizations have to be designed to fight and motivated to win; communications are required to co-ordinate the deployment and employment of resources; and logistics are needed to move the product to the market-place and to deploy sales and service forces. Neglecting the value, development or use of any of these support elements and fighting against a competitor with qualitative and quantitative superiority in weaponry, intelligence, organization and leadership, communications and logistics is a formula for failure.

Source References

1.   Business Week, July 7 and August 18, 1980.

2.   Fortune, October 5, 1981.

3.   Forbes, September 28, 1981.

4.   The Economist, April 26, 1980.

5.   McKinsey Quarterly, Spring, 1981.

6.   op. cit. McKinsey Quarterly.

7.   New York, March 28, 1983.

8.   Business Week, July 11, 1983 and June 4, 1984.

9.   Fortune, September 24, 1979.

10. The Economist, November 8, 1980.

11. The Economist, November 1, 1980.

12. The Economist, July 28, 1984.

13. Business Week, September 1, 1980.

14. The Wall Street Journal, February 22, 1983.

15. AMA Management Review, March, 1980.

16. *op. cit. AMA Management Review*

17. The Wall Street Journal, October 31, 1983.

18. The Economist, November 8, 1980.

19. Business Week, September 1, 1980.

20. The Economist, November 1, 1980.

21. Fortune, July 26, 1982.

22. World Business Weekly, September 28, 1981.

23. Fortune, May 14, 1984.

24. The Wall Street Journal, July 23, 1982.

25. The Wall Street Journal, August 5, 1982.

26. The Wall Street Journal, August 27, 1984.

27. Business Week, September 8,. 1980.

28. Business Week, October 13, 1980.

29. Business Week, December 10, 1979.

30. Business Week, July 11, 1983.

31. The Economist, January 31, 1981.

32. The Wall Street Journal, November 1, 1983.

33. Fortune, February 23, 1981.

34. Business Week, March 19, 1984.

35. Fortune, December 12, 1983 and The Economist July 21, 1984.

36. Fortune, March 8, 1982.

37. Business Week, July 21, 1980.

38. *op. cit. Business Week*

39. Business Week, October 27, 1980.

40. The Wall Street Journal, April 9, 1982.

41. Business Week, May 18, 1981.

42. Fortune, November 16, 1981.

43. The Wall Street Journal, November 11, 1982.

44. The Wall Street Journal, September 1, 1981.

45. The Financial Times, March 10, 1983.

chapter eight
THE REALITIES OF COMBAT

> Summers: 'You know, you never did beat us on the battlefield'.
> Reply: 'That may be so, but it is also irrelevant'.
> > Conversation between Colonel Harry Summers, US Army,
> > and a North Vietnamese Colonel. Hanoi (1975)

It is hardly surprising, given the similarities in organizational concepts, competitive systems and strategic manœuvres, that companies and armies exhibit the same unerring ability to ignore the basic realities of combat.

This chapter identifies the key failures to appreciate the fundamental rules of conflict; explores the misconceptions of formulae and simulation approaches to combat; and concludes by suggesting that the key to success in the market–place depends on the ability of companies to select and implement strategies which truly emphasize the nature of conflict.

COMBAT REALITIES

Companies and armies fail in combat in the market–place and on the battlefield because they invariably overlook a number of simple ground rules which have been tested and proved time and again.

Preparing to fight the last war rather than preparing to fight the next war.
The analysis of past success and failure is an obvious strategy to avoid making the same mistakes; however, the enemy, the environment, tactics and weaponry have an unfortunate tendency to change, altering the ground rules for the next engagement.

The Luftwaffe was fought to a standstill by the RAF in the Battle of Britain (1940) since it used the same strategy which had been successfully employed in the Spanish Civil War and in invasions of Poland, Denmark, the Low Countries and France. The Luftwaffe failed to appreciate the differences in quality and quantity of opposing pilots and aircraft, of operating at extreme fighter range over hostile territory and over the sea, and of the effective use of radar by the RAF.

The Swiss watch industry almost fatally misjudged the market-place for watches in the early 1970s. With huge economies of scale in manufacturing mechanical movements, the leading Swiss companies ASUAG and SSIH, decided not to make the transition to electronic movements. The electronic watch offered vastly greater economics than mechanical movements and a range of new competitors emerged who were able to enter the market, drive down prices and open up a huge volume market with fashionable, gadget-laden, almost disposable, watches. The Swiss companies, with a strategy based solely on the conventional wisdom of the old market, image, lost almost 70% of their market share by 1983 to companies who developed a new market based on price and fashion.

Valspar lost its traditional leadership of the UK paint market in the late 1950s by failing to anticipate the rise of the do-it-yourself market. ICI, a distant second, nurtured this new market. By opening up new distribution channels to retail outlets and using heavy consumer promotion to build strong brand awareness ICI out-manœuvred Valspar, who continued to promote heavily to decorators and building supplies outlets, a declining segment of the market. ICI became brand leader by 1958 as a result of Valspar's preoccupation with fighting the old war to win decorator sales rather than trying to win the new war of consumer sales.

Past success is no guarantee of future success. More of the same is rarely the answer, for any length of time, in military or business combat. However, the successful lessons of the past are frequently elevated to eternal myths which are hard to shatter.

Concentrating on fighting for the objective rather than on fighting the enemy.
A fortified position or a market share can only be secured if the opponent is overwhelmed; otherwise the position constantly remains vulnerable to an enemy attack and any position or a market share, even if secured, runs a risk if it is under constant attack.

By 1812 Napoleon had virtually cut England off from the Continent with the sole exception of Russia. For the first time Napoleon allowed politics to intrude on strategy by deciding to occupy Moscow to force the Tsar to terms. By focusing on the occupation of a geographic point instead of the destruction of his enemy's army, Napoleon was faced with a formidable war against extended French communications. Within a short time the Grande Armée was forced to retreat from Russia.

Companies with dominant market shares in low growth markets, termed 'Cash Cows', have adopted the formula approach of milking their products for profit. Companies wedded to Cash Cow tactics have been vanquished by aggressive competitors who single-mindedly concentrate on market penetration and later take their profits, as the Cash Cow companies continue to focus on the results of their previous market domination rather than fighting to keep their market shares. Honda, using the cash flows from its successful penetration of the US motorcycle market, financed a seven year programme to enter and develop the small-size European markets. Honda turned market preference around to its own products by investing heavily in distribution, service support and consumer advertising. Honda moved customers up the model range to larger margin motorcycles and expanded into a full line of motorcycles which increased volume and reduced marketing and distribution costs. The higher volume translated into economies of scale in marketing and production — a feature that escaped the competition with modest volumes. By the mid-1970s Honda was the major factor in the European motorcycle market.[1]

In contrast, Sony became enamoured with its innovative capability in the mid-1970s and neglected to develop strategies which fully integrated its technological leadership into a cohesive competitive policy. While Sony was highly successful as a product innovator and was able to charge premium prices, this strategy was viable only as long as Sony could maintain a two to three year technological monopoly. When Sony's technological lead-time shrank to four to eight months as competitors became more proficient at duplicating Sony's innovations, the premium pricing policy provided Hitachi, Matsushita, Sharp, and Toshiba, who had concentrated on rapid product development and low cost production, with the opportunity to quickly market 'me-too' products of comparable quality at lower prices. From the end of the 1970s, Sony began to falter as its Betamax VTR, SMC-70 personal computer and word processor all failed to achieve or maintain strong market positions as a result of Sony's fixation on technological leadership at the expense of an integrated competitive policy.

Armies and companies are frequently deflected from their true mission — the defeat of the enemy — by the immediate and more visible results of success, — temporary battlefield or market domination — which are often translated into personal executive advancement.

Underestimating the magnitude of the task and overestimating capabilities

Combat, whether offensive or defensive, can be costly, particularly if a combatant misjudges the resources required and the conflict turns into a war of attrition.

The Wehrmacht, while outstandingly successful in the initial attack on Russia (1941) which brought them to the gates of Moscow, totally underestimated the task of subduing Russia. The formidable winter, extended lines of communications in a hostile environment, the resolve of a nation fighting on its own territory, the transfer of Russian war production to protected locations East of the Urals, Allied material aid and a war on two fronts combined to make the Wehrmacht's position untenable.

Biotechnologies Inc., Lee Biomolecular Research and Southern Biotech all went bankrupt in the US in 1982. These firms underestimated the time and cost of bringing products of a new technology, genetic engineering, to the market to create an income stream to support their small capital bases.[2] Similarly John De Lorean underestimated the time and cost of bringing his sports car to the market and overestimated the size of the market and De Lorean Motors' ability to raise additional capital. De Lorean went into liquidation in Northern Ireland in 1981. Magnuson Computer Systems, a manufacturer of medium-sized IBM-compatible computers, became very successful in the late 1970s when IBM was unable to supply a new model. IBM reduced prices in 1981 and introduced a new model, and in 1982 added two further models and again reduced prices. Magnuson overestimated its ability to maintain its position in the market which was obtained by competitive default rather than by imaginative strategies and lacked the resources for a full-scale war of attrition with IBM. Magnuson went bankrupt in early 1983. Royal Crown Cola (RC) is probably the most innovative company in the US soft drinks market. Three times RC introduced new products which created major new market segments. Diet Rite, a diet cola introduced in 1962, RC100 a caffeine-free cola in 1980 and RC100 Regular a caffeine-free diet cola in 1982 were all major new product innovations. Coca-Cola and Pepsi-Cola captured most of the market segments pioneered by RC since RC was unable to compete effectively against the huge resources of the market leaders who were able to outpromote, outdistribute and outdiscount RC throughout the market-place. By 1982 the pioneer RC languished in ninth place in the US soft drinks market with a 2.6% share — one tenth of the market share of Coca-Cola or Pepsi-Cola.

In any combat situation a keen sense of judgment is required to balance intent with resources. Taking on more than can be handled with limited resources can be disastrous. In wars of attrition the one with the more limited resources is invariably the loser.

Relying on size and resources rather than mobility and speed to win battles.

Armies and companies have been consistently outmanœuvred on the battlefield and in the market-place by small, aggressive, competitors. Bulk slows down the response time to a challenge enabling the small, but mobile, aggressor to secure the advantage.

Frederick the Great successfully used mobility and speed allied with superior training to overcome his limited resources in the face of, invariably, numerically superior enemies. In successive wars, the Israelis have consistently outmanœuvred the larger combined armed forces of Egypt, Iraq, Jordan and Syria with aggressive strategies emphasizing mobility and speed.

Chantiers Bénéteau a small French boat-builder, rose from the brink of bankruptcy to lead the sailing boat market in Europe by using a strategy emphasizing mobility. Bénéteau realized that by moving to independent distributors interested in selling boats and by developing mass-market boats capable of generating high volumes, economies of scale could be used to keep prices low. Bénéteau was highly successful since its once larger competitors relied on high commission sales direct from the boat-yard and on high priced high performance boats, both of which contrasted with the volume opportunities available to Bénéteau through its product and distribution strategies.[3]

BMW also came back from the brink of bankruptcy in 1960 to become one of the leading quality car manufacturers using speed and mobility to win a significant stake in the world car market. BMW identified the sporty saloon car market as an area untapped by its major and much larger rival in Germany, Mercedes. BMW evolved a line of high quality cars with better performance and a more sporty image than Mercedes or any other manufacturer. Following the successful introduction of the 1500 model in 1961, BMW launched the 1800 in 1963 and again became profitable. By 1969, BMW had overhauled Mercedes in sales of petrol-engine cars in Germany and by the mid-1970s, continuing to rely on mobility with constant model improvement and evolution, BMW had become a major factor world-wide in the quality sporting saloon car market. BMW's continued focus on constant model improvement and quality has enabled the company to successfully ride out the two OPEC price increases, the economic recession, and the world wide slump in car sales. By 1983 BMW had reached sales of $5.5 billion and profits of $106 million and was sustaining an annual growth rate of 20%.[4]

In contrast, the large UK packaged food companies, such as Brooke Bond, Cadbury-Schweppes, Huntley & Palmer, Lyons and Unigate, which possessed considerable business skills and marketing and financial muscle, were unable to secure a significant share of many food markets in Europe in the 1960s. Small local companies were able to successfully defend their markets through a mobile defensive strategy which emphasized their experience and knowledge of market conditions and consumer needs. This ultimately forced the closure or write off of parts of the Eurpean operations of all these UK companies who were unable to compete with their smaller and more mobile competitors.

Rapid reaction time is essential to foil the attempts of aggressors to gain the initiative. It is always more costly to dislodge an entrenched competitor than it is to deter a potential aggressor.

Being unprepared for combat
Throughout history, armies and companies have failed to see the build-up of resources of a potential aggressor and have been unable to effectively counter early moves by competitors.

The British were completely unprepared to resist the Argentine invasion of the Falklands (1982) even though there was considerable diplomatic, satellite, signal intercept and covert intelligence to suggest the imminence of an attack.

The Woolworths chain store failed, in both the US and UK, to spot, and respond quickly to, demographic shifts of households to the suburbs. This increased operating costs and lost them customers to suburban shopping centres and to competition from discount chains who offered higher quality products at lower prices. Within a few years Woolworths was transformed from a retail leader into an industry laggard in both countries by being unprepared for environmental and competitive shifts.[5]

Philip Morris in the United States failed to identify that R.J. Reynold's low tar cigarette Cambridge, would satisfy a rapidly expanding market need. Philip Morris took four years to evaluate the competitive product and its strategy, and the low tar market segment by which time Cambridge had built such a strong brand franchise that Philip Morris' own belated and unsuccessful brand entry incurred over $100 million in launch costs.[6]

BAC introduced the One-Eleven, the first short-haul twin-jet airliner, in 1965, several years ahead of the rival Boeing 737 and McDonnell-Douglas DC-9. Although the early introduction and large orders from American Airlines, Braniff and Mohawk placed the One-Eleven in the lead, BAC was completely unprepared for the competitive product development policies of its rivals and stuck too long to an aircraft that had limited passenger capacity. When BAC finally introduced the stretched 500 model in 1968, it was too late as the major airlines had already ordered the larger capacity 737 and DC-9 in volume. In 1982 BAe, as BAC had become, stopped production of the One-Eleven at 230 aircraft and transferred production to Rumania while the rival 737 and DC-9 remained in production with orders (at the end of 1983) of 1,071 and 1,200 aircraft respectively.

Territory, whether land or market share, is a coveted possession and a high degree of vigilance is required to avoid a surprise attack. The adage 'do it to others before it is done to you' is relevant to both the general and the executive. In both war and business few victories are finite and vigilance is necessary to safeguard against the ephemeral nature of combat.

Following traditional, rather than new and creative strategies.
Considerable amounts of time and effort are put into evaluating strategies, but considerably less entrepreneurial effort is devoted to generating truly new ideas to give a unit a combat edge.

While the Romans were almost unbeatable on land, they failed for many years to challenge Carthage at sea. The Romans realized that they could not hope to equal Carthage as long as they themselves used traditional naval tactics of the day. The Romans devised new tactics using flexible boarding bridges to enable the superiority of their soldiers in hand-to-hand combat to have full scope. At Mylae (260 BC) the Romans' new tactics proved decisive against Carthage.

The Air Products Company revolutionized the industrial gases market in the 1940s in the USA by choosing a manufacturing and distribution strategy which was completely opposite to that used by the industry. Rather than follow the industry's traditional strategy of building large-scale centralized plants to give economies of scale, Air Products built small, localized plants close to the facilities of its largest customers. By using a new and creative strategy which provided high levels of service and low distribution costs from its localized plants, Air Products were able to lock out its competitors from a major share of the US industrial gases market.[7] Cessna at one time held 67% of the Brazilian light aircraft market, compared to its largest rival, Piper's, 17% share. Embraer, a Brazilian government company, invited Cessna and Piper to propose assembly agreements for light planes supplied in kit form. Cessna was inflexible in negotiations and Piper, recognizing the advantages of a large local government-backed company, offered a creative proposal. Piper became the exclusive supplier to Embraer. As a result of import barriers erected to protect Embraer, Cessna has sold no light planes to Brazil since 1974 and Piper now holds 100% of the market.[8]

The conventional wisdom in the home computer market was that buyers needed 'hand-holding' from specialist retailers like Computer-Land who knew how computers worked. Commodore defied traditional orthodoxy and used mass merchandizers in the US like K-Mart, Toys 'R' Us, Target and others to market Commodores' machines at low prices for the class — around $200. Commodores' unconventional strategy for the 64 model was a phenomenal success and pushed Commodores' unit share of the home computer market from 25% in 1983 to 55% in 1984 which increased Commodores' value share of the $2 billion home computer market to 38%.[9]

In the glutted second-hand commercial airliner market in 1982 McDonnell-Douglas took an unusual step to moderate the slack in the sales of the DC-9-80. McDonnell-Douglas began to offer leasing rather than sales deals to airlines and quickly signed American Airlines to a five year rental arrangement including a formula to share profits derived from operating the new planes.

This innovative approach quickly attracted other customers including Alitalia and TWA, and pushed back the prospects of a new 150-seat airliner which was being contemplated by its main rivals Airbus and Boeing.

The unorthodox approach to combat has a consistently high level of success in war and business. While traditional strategies are tried and true, they cannot accommodate the unorthodox which institutes new ground rules for combat.

Choosing the wrong enemy at the wrong time, in the wrong place.
A key to successful combat is the skill in choosing the battleground and the enemy to provide the attacker or the defender with the advantage.

The RCA and Xerox challenges to IBM in the mainframe computer market typify choosing the wrong competitor in the wrong market. IBM was entrenched in a strong defensive position in terms of resources, reputation and technological prowess. Both competitors had limited resources available for this expensive venture, were forced to create an image from scratch, and could not match the technological, service and marketing skills of IBM. The result was the eventual withdrawl of both companies from the computer mainframe business.

AEG-Telefunken, West Germany's largest electronics manufacturer was brought to the brink of bankruptcy in mid-1982 as a result of AEG's continuously poor choice of enemies and battle-grounds. In the 1960s AEG fought and lost a battle against Italian companies, led by Zanussi, in the durable domestic appliance markets in Europe. In the 1970s, AEG fought an equally disastrous engagement in the European consumer electronics market against the Japanese. While the other major West German electronics companies such as Siemens, concentrated on the electrical capital goods market where they were less vulnerable to competition, AEG concentrated on fighting in the consumer electronics market where its vulnerability was high and its slow reaction time to competitive attacks proved almost fatal.[10]

The major US chemical companies faced with stagnating or declining demand for their bulk low margin commodity chemicals in the late 1970s, identified W.R. Grace's successful early diversification into high margin speciality chemicals and decided to follow suit. While the major chemical companies had correctly identified strong growth markets with significant profit opportunities, they seriously underestimated the competition, the timing, and the market. The market was dominated by subsidiaries of large diversified companies with considerable financial and marketing muscle. Grace had evolved its position over time and there were few significant acquisitions candidates available; the market segments of the speciality chemical business were relatively small. Faced with these conditions, the major chemical companies reduced the scale of their attack and looked for more promising targets.

A cardinal rule in any form of combat is to fight only when you have the advantage or can at least engineer a situation where the success factors outweigh the risks and those risks are predictable and can be contained without destroying the organization. While Montgomery was frequently criticized for not being as aggressive as his American counterparts in World War II, Montgomery ranks with Marlborough in never having beseiged a city that he did not take, nor fighting a battle that he did not win.

Static situations invariably lead to neglect of combat efficiency.
Lulls in combat have almost always led to a degradation of combat capability, preparedness, training, morale and in the quality and quantity of the weaponry.

The combined Belgian, British, Dutch and French armed forces were numerically superior to the Germans in 1940 and in certain respects had limited quantities of superior weapons. However, the Allies were unable to match the training, morale and preparedness of the Germans, and were quickly defeated.

Kellogg had dominated the US breakfast cereal market so thoroughly for so long that it began to neglect the market-place. As market growth shrank in the late 1970s, General Mills, General Foods and Quaker Oats, through aggressive price promotion, coupons and the launch of a number of new products made gains at a lethargic Kellogg's expense, reducing the firm's commanding market share from 41% in 1979 to 38% in 1982.

Penguin Books, the largest paperback book publisher in the UK, began to lose out to competition in 1970 and by the late 1970s had not only lost market share, but had increased its debts and overheads and was in a loss-making situation. As a complacent market leader over time, Penguin had lost touch with the mass market on which its fortunes had been built. Penguin was finally turned around in 1981 through a combination of a major reorganization, including a change of management, cost cutting and aggressive marketing. Penguin reduced the number of new titles introduced, sought out new authors and titles at premium prices, and adopted a variety of flexible formats to exploit its biggest asset — a formidable backlist of titles — all aimed at the mass market. By 1982, Penguin had regained its leadership position with a 25% market share and was one of only four profitable paperback publishers in the UK.[11]

No army or firm can function effectively if it is ill-prepared for the task. The fact that many armies and companies in a static position have been decimated by aggressors through neglect brought on by complacency, indicates that continuous upgrading of combat capability is essential for survival.

The discontinuity of combat.

Winning one engagement does not win a war, and a combatant must expect that a challenge will be mounted at any time. Fortunes ebb and flow over time as conditions change. Throughout military history the victory-defeat-victory cycle has dogged all armies as they advance, retreat and advance in response to changing conditions.

There are similar parallels in business combat. The pace of technological change in electronics has been so radical that in the evolution from valves to transistors, to semiconductors, to integrated circuits, only one firm, RCA, has been able to maintain a significant market share in all phases of evolution. Each phase of the electronics evolution has been spearheaded by new competitors who have largely displaced the leaders of the previous phase, who were unable to follow through with effective innovation.[12]

From 36 certified airlines prior to de-regulation in 1978 the US airline industry grew to 125 airlines by mid-1984; however, over the five year period 28 airlines went out of business as a result of the high levels of competition introduced by de-regulation including discounting fares to uneconomic levels and excess passenger capacity.[13]

Savin, in 1975, marketing small, inexpensive, photocopiers from Ricoh of Japan, caught the leader, Xerox, off guard and the appeal of Savin's machines enabled the company to grow explosively at Xerox' expense. However, by 1983, Savin lost its exclusive right to market Ricoh's machines and would lose all US rights by 1985. Savin was faced with the need to invest heavily ($80 to $90 million) in its own manufacturing plant to continue selling photocopiers at a time when Xerox was dropping prices aggressively to match the high growth, lower price end of the market which was being simultaneously attacked by Canon, Sharp and IBM.[14]

Heavy price discounting of their tickets became a normal situation for airlines in the air travel market. Although discounting had been around for a long time, the airlines, with overcapacity and a slow growth in passenger traffic, began to discount tickets at rates substantially below the official rates to special discount or 'bucket' shops in the late 1970s. By 1982, the market had reached an estimated one billion dollars — the difference between the discount rates and the official tariffs. The airlines were confronted by a major revenue drain from the discounted tickets, angry reactions from the traditional travel agents who were losing business, and the effects of the recession which had brought traffic declines on many routes. The airlines strategy of filling empty seats at almost any price rather than having spare capacity had eventually backfired.[15]

General Motors (GM) with a range of diesel cars was the only US car manufacturer able to tap the explosive growth in demand for diesel engined cars in the US in the late 1970s following the OPEC price increases. The promise of better mileage at diesel fuel prices, which were slightly less than that of petrol, pushed the market in 1981 to over 500,000 units, just over 6% of the US car market, with GM taking over 50% of the market at premium prices. Eventually a combination of premium prices, poor acceleration, noisy operation and poor quality and the drop in petrol prices to a few cents less than diesel fuel per gallon shrank the US diesel car market to 150,000 units, around 1.6% of the market, by 1983.

GM, unable to solve its mechanical and quality problems saw its market share fall to 23% — a volume decline of over 80% in three years.[16]

Armies and companies need the resources, coupled with a flexible organization, to successfully deal with the discontinuity of combat.

The inability to concede an engagement
The inability of both army commanders and company executives to face up to the fact that they are losing an engagement is one of the most critical factors in both forms of combat. For behavioural reasons, armies and firms have a knack of not knowing when to

retreat from a situation which could have crippling effects on the organization.

General Galtieri, when faced with the real prospect of war with Britain after the Argentine occupation of the Falklands in 1982, was unable to back down without the real threat of his government falling. Following the Argentine defeat, the Galtieri-led junta collapsed. Similarly, once the Royal Navy task-force put to sea, Mrs. Thatcher was faced with the prospect of fighting to reoccupy the Falklands, since it was unlikely that the Argentines would voluntarily withdraw, or of facing the probable demise of her government if the fleet was recalled.

Hugh Hefner's strategy for Playboy Enterprises was to expand widely into ventures which supported the life-style concept espoused in Playboy magazine. By 1981, Playboy had interests in clubs, resort hotels, films, television shows, recording, book publishing, gambling, licensing and a second magazine, Oui. Only Playboy magazine, the gambling interests and the licensing activities were profitable and the remaining businesses were losing money. Hefner was reluctant to sell off these loss-makers since they were part of the overall 'strategic' image of Playboy Enterprises. The loss of the UK gambling licenses in 1981, which provided most of the company's profits, and the inability of Playboy to secure a New Jersey gambling license forced Hefner to divest the company of book publishing and recording operations and two resort hotels, to remain afloat. At the same time Hefner changed the operating management and became less involved in directing the business.[17]

It is just as important to know when not to fight as when to fight. However, once committed to combat, the political options of most commanders or executives narrow, and the choices adopted tend towards the political rather than the operational realities of combat.

While these combat realities may appear trite and obvious, the fact that they have been overlooked so frequently on the battlefield and in the market-place, with equally disastrous results, suggests that reality may not always be obvious. The realities of combat are being consistently validated; however, time after time, old lessons in strategy are ignored, which is, in itself, another lesson that repeatedly gets validated.

FORMULA APPROACHES

'There is no 'science' of war, and there never will be any. There are
many sciences war is concerned with. But war itself is not a science;
war is practical art and skill'.

Leon Trotsky (1924)

Armies and companies have widely adopted the formula approach
to strategy as a means to gain a combat edge.

The modified Schlieffen plan for an offensive war in the West and
a defensive war in the East, although vindicated on the Eastern
front at Tannenberg (1914), was a disaster on the Western front. The
wheeling right wing through Belgium to completely encircle the
French army lacked the strength to complete the manœuvre and
since the French were not strong enough in the South to overcome
the Germans, the war turned into a stalemate. The Blitzkrieg
concept, embodying aircraft, tanks and motorized infantry, relied
on concentration and speed to throw the enemy off balance;
surprise to breed shock; shock leading to the disintegration,
collapse of morale and retreat of the enemy forces. While this
formula was highly effective in Poland (1939) and France (1940) it
failed in the Ardennes (1944) since the Germans faced a well armed
and well led foe with complete air supremacy.

In business combat, companies have relied on sophisticated
formulae to win battles in the market-place. Many industrial goods
companies have successfully used the Boston Consulting Group's
Experience Curve strategy which is designed to achieve; 1. overall
cost leadership in an industry through aggressive use of efficiency;
2. cost reductions through experience as workers become more
adept, machines more efficient and improvements are made to the
manufacturing system; and 3. tight control of expenditures and
capital investment. While Texas Instruments (TI) used this formula
with great success in its industrial electronics business with
semiconductors it failed completely when applying the formula to
consumer electronics such as electronic watches and home
computers as TI concentrated on selling technology rather than on
meeting consumer needs.[18] In all markets customers do not buy
technology they buy the expected benefits those technologies will
bring to them.

In the 1920s Ford had achieved cost leadership in the US car market through automation and a limited model range. When incomes rose and customers began to place premiums on style and variety, General Motors, with its annual body styling change and a range of models and options, easily outmanœuvred Ford's single-minded formula approach to market–place combat.[19] In essence both TI and Ford tried to sell what they could make rather than making what they could sell — with inevitable results.

In a number of industries the Experience Curve concept is virtually useless. For example, in the pharmaceutical industry the savings which can be made from increased cumulative production volumes for prescription drugs are insignificant and the Experience Curve is almost flat. Experience Curve strategies appear particularly suited to commodity markets where costs and price are critical. However, there are few markets which truly fit this pattern. Almost all products have features which provide for a differentiation from competing products. Even products widely regarded as commodities such as coal and steel, have differentiating factors such as grade or quality, availability and packaging, all of which can change the attitude of the consumer to different offerings. In most cases, while the product may be outwardly similar, the values attached by the market–place are widely disparate. A further flaw in the Experience Curve concept is that volume produced has to be sold and in situations of declining industrial and consumer demand, production either has to decline in line with demand or inventories have to increase to accommodate over–production. Both options lead to increased unit cost. While it can be argued that all competitors' unit costs move up as demand slows or declines, the strategic issue changes from one of producing goods at the lowest cost to selling output profitably.

Other popular formula approaches in business include Shell's Directional Policy Matrix, the Boston Consulting Group's Growth/Share Matrix and Business Portfolio, the Strategic Planning Institute's PIMS (Profit Impact of Market Strategies), and General Electric's Business Screen. All of these concepts seek to assess profit and growth prospects, and business strengths and weaknesses, as a means to balance resources. A number of firms have succumbed to the frailty of these formulae.

Companies with large market shares in static or low growth markets (Cash Cows) have adopted policies of harvesting profits rather than of defending their market shares. Yamaha successfully destroyed the dominance of the well-established US musical instrument manufacturers who concentrated on milking their products for profit in a mature market rather than on fighting a defensive battle to maintain their market shares.[20] Products with a small share and with little or no growth, termed 'Dogs', should, according to Portfolio theory, be abandoned. This discounts the valuable strategic moves that are frequently made with Dog products or ventures where the primary aim is not maximizing profit as such, but, for example, to provide economies of scale in manufacturing, marketing and administration to sustain the overall business. The primary aim of Caterpillar's joint venture with Mitsubishi in Japan in the mid-1960s was to pressure its major competitor, Komatsu, in its home market where Komatsu derived 80% of its world-wide cash flow. While Caterpillar's joint venture was a distant second in the market for construction equipment in Japan and was not highly profitable, the joint venture served as a strategic break on Komatsu's international expansion since Komatsu was constantly faced with a need to defend itself in its home market.[21]

Similarly Portfolio theory does not value the fighting brand approach. Clorox' introduction of Wave into the US domestic bleach market was designed to deflect Procter & Gamble's attack on the market leader, Clorox, by creating a 'second front' in the market rather than to generate substantial profits from Wave.[22] Also damning to the Portfolio theory is the fact that businesses in classic Dog situations, with low shares in stagnant commodity-type markets can make greater profits than the market leaders. Republic Gypsum in the USA is a small one-plant manufacturer of wallboards with 1982 sales of $20 million and a 2% share of the US plasterboard market. Republic is very distant from the leaders, 37% (US Gypsum's) and 27% (National Gypsum's), market shares. Republic concentrates on a small sales area centered on Oklahoma and North Texas. Reliant on the construction industry, Republic adjusts the sales radius to adjacent areas meeting local prices and absorbs high freight:product costs with its own trucking fleet. Republic owns a wholesale building supplies company in Dallas and integrates trucking and storage to reduce freight costs of plasterboard. The major competitors cannot enlarge territories without cannibalizing the sales area of one of their own plants and use contract freight carriers at high costs. Republic, with 94% plant utilization in 1982 against 70% for the rest of the industry, achieved operating margins after depreciation of 13.5% — triple that of US Gypsum and almost quadruple that of National Gypsum.[23]

The PIMS programme has also been widely used as a strategic tool. PIMS compares various operating characteristics of a company with other companies exhibiting similar characteristics such as investment intensity, market share and vertical integration, in a database which has been assembled empirically using linear regression analysis based on input from several thousand companies. The PIMS behavioural model suggests that just 9 factors determine 80% of the variances in operating results of businesses in the database. The PIMS programme is based on a number of assumptions. PIMS assumes that businesses generally behave in a regular and predictable manner and that all businesses are alike in obeying the same laws of the market-place. This suggests that a competitor adopting an innovative approach which goes against the rules of the market-place cannot succeed. The 25% prescription market share of the US ethical drug market taken in 1982 by companies marketing generic (low priced, off-patent) drugs against the original but higher priced branded drugs was obtained by companies adopting an approach which went against the traditional laws of the market. PIMS also assumes that product characteristics do not matter. The Japanese car companies succeeded in obtaining a large share of the world car market by offering better quality cars with innovative standard features at highly competitive prices. None of the nine major strategic influences on profitability and net cash flow which PIMS suggest are key elements feature the quality of management, logistics, communications, legislation or customer perceptions.

Generic formulae approaches to market combat also fail because they are single-minded and do not totally integrate the resources of the firm. For years the motorcycle manufacturers in the US and Western Europe milked their products for profit in a stagnant market. When faced with a concerted challenge from Honda, Kawasaki, Suzuki and Yamaha, the incumbent manufacturers relied almost entirely on quality and reputation to fend off attack and continued to harvest profits. The challengers used a totally integrated strategy which utilized all their strengths and skills: by building fully stocked distribution and fully trained service networks; using economies of scale and tight quality control to provide high quality, low-cost products. With this, and backed by financial resources which enabled heavy volume consumer promotion and rapid model changes to continually attract customers, the challengers were able to mount large-scale market penetration strategies aimed at securing initial high shares with delayed profit taking. The market shares of the incumbents were devastated by these integrated strategies.

The formulae do not focus adequately on the basic functions and operating skills that are at the core of a firm's business strengths. The technologies used by a firm; the products and services produced, distributed and marketed; the firm's relationships with customers, suppliers, governments and the financial community; and the firm's financial and human resources are all key operating functions. Companies derive their relative combat strengths from the way in which management strikes a balance between its relative skills in each of the functions and the way in which this balance is fine-tuned to meet the demands of the market-place. Few strategic formulae integrate more than one or two of the core skills into a central strategic theme. The result, far too often, is an iceberg strategy which leaves the bulk of the firm's skills submerged and not integrated into the central strategic theme. While generic formulae are useful as analytical tools to indicate the relative position of the company, and to view disparate businesses in a multi-market company in a logical manner, and can identify strategic options, they cannot determine which is the best possible strategic option or how to implement a strategy which utilizes all the strengths and skills of the firm. Applying stereotype strategies based on analytical models are not much use when a competitor, using a different set of data, reacts unconventionally and completely changes the rules of the game.

SIMULATION

'It is simply not possible to construct a model for the art of war since models create an absurd difference between theory and practice'.

Carl von Clausewitz.

Several methods have been adopted by the military and business to overcome the sterile nature of plans and models by attempting to replicate combat conditions to help design strategic alternatives.

In the military, wargaming, and more recently the use of computer graphics, have brought the simulation of combat conditions to a fine art. The USAF, under the Red Flag programme at Nellis Air Force base in Nevada, used the 64th Fighter Weapons Squadron to simulate air–to–air combat. The aggressor squadron, equipped with Northrop F5E fighters and reputedly with covertly acquired Russian Mig-21 and -23 aircraft complete with Russian markings, and using Russian air combat techniques, provides USAF pilots with dogfight simulation.

In business, game theory based on the mathematical theory of the behaviour of parties in conflict situations (developed by von Neumann and Morgenstern in the late 1940s) and the case study method developed at the Harvard Business School, have been used in an attempt to simulate market combat conditions. More recently, computers have been used to translate complex concepts into explicit dynamic models of market behaviour to simulate the reaction of the market–place to change, and financial and econometric models have been developed to simulate corporate financial options and to forecast national supply and demand trends. In practice, sophisticated plans, models and simulation have major drawbacks since there are very real gaps between theory and practice. By its very nature, combat involves dealing with discontinuity. The flexibility of combat on the battlefield and in the market–place is such that all preconceived plans and models prove less than effective under operational conditions. The success of any plan depends entirely on the actual, and not on the assumed response of an opponent and on environmental conditions. Both are governed by conditions not under the control of any army or company. Put succinctly by von Moltke the Elder, 'No plan survives contact with the enemy'.

Military combat simulation, or wargaming, is, however, much more advanced conceptually than that of business simulation. The military has long accepted the 'Wild Card' theory — a term used to describe an unpredictable event likely to have far reaching effects on the outcome of a conflict. Business, in general, does not appear to accept that an unpredictable event can occur which can change the outcome of a conflict in the market–place. National Cash Register (NCR) for many years led the cash register business in the USA with its electro–mechanical units, but failed to move rapidly into the market with electronic cash registers. Burroughs exploited both its expertise in electronics and NCR's failure to foresee a technology shift and took market leadership from NCR. Similarly, the Japanese gained a beachhead in the US semiconductor market during the 1973—1975 recession by having excess production capability when their US competitors did not. By 1978, the US manufacturers could not keep up with demand due to their reluctance to invest in new production capacity and techniques in the recessionary period, while their Japanese counterparts had continued to invest in production. At the end of 1979, some 42% of the US 16K RAM chip market was held by Japanese companies who had taken the initiative to continuously invest in production which provided a quantity and quality edge over their US competitors who were over cautious. While business simulation uses the 'What if' factor to provide alternative scenarios, these factors are limited to changes in productive capacity, cost, price and marketing expenditure and do not accommodate unorthodox competitive strategic approaches, the appearance of new competitors or radical shifts in technology, consumer preferences, legislation and underlying social, political and economic conditions.

Although both armies and firms are institutions which resemble their opponents, they are different since each is a mirror of its own society and that society's values and objectives. As no two societies are mirror images of each other it is difficult to predict the response to combat manœuvres, and to construct models and formulate plans to accommodate all variations. Sophisticated Portfolio and Experience Curve strategies, for example, have been devastated by Japanese firms using the simplistic strategy of market penetration, in industries as diverse as cameras, cars, hi-fi, motorcycles, ships, steel, television sets and zip fasteners. Formula approaches also are time-limited since what may be appropriate now can be totally wrong in the future as a result of environmental volatility. Models fail under combat conditions since they cannot accommodate random change. Similarly, simulation fails since it cannot truly replicate the realities of combat in terms of pressure, risk and opponent reaction. No simulation can provide the realism of the noise, heat, smoke and disorientation which accompanies conflict on the battlefield and in the market-place. While formulae are useful for analysis and for looking at markets and competitors in new ways, and while models and simulation can help to prepare for combat, they are a means to an end and not an end in themselves.

Winning strategies do not emerge from formulae and models and simulation will not prove a strategy's value. Entrepreneurial skills are needed to develop winning strategies and combat experience is essential to implement winning strategies. Simply, you cannot win if you do not have a sound strategy and equally, strategies that cannot be implemented are useless.

COMBAT: THE ESSENCE OF CONFLICT.

'I know there exist many good men who honestly believe that one may, by the aid of modern science, sit in comfort and ease in his office chair, and, with figures and algebraic symbols, master the great game of war. I think that is an insidious and most dangerous mistake'.

General William Tecumsah Sherman (1869)

The military, and to an even larger extent business, have embraced the armchair concept of combat in the mistaken belief that they can plan, model and simulate their way out of trouble and on to victory.

Formulae and simulation approaches to strategy have been widely adopted by business for two reasons. Firstly, for a hundred years since Frederick Taylor's work in the 1880s, business has had a love affair with the precision of the rational and numerical approach of Scientific Management and has readily embraced new theories predicated on quantitative decision making techniques. Under these conditions it was easy for a community of strategy intellectuals to develop and sell a body of theory and literacy characterized by a cool analytical approach to business. Secondly, for thirty years from 1945 business enjoyed almost continuous non-inflationary growth and it was arguably easier to gain market share under these conditions than in the low growth, mature or declining markets of the 1980s. This in turn contributed to the 'success' image of the formulae and simulation theories. Little wonder that business easily succumbed to the elegance of the formulae and simulation theories in the late 1960s and 1970s which neatly boxed complex strategic problems with simple solutions in an attractive package. Pre-conditioning and success are hard to beat.

Companies, like armies, have been deluding themselves by imagining that the combination of weapons technology in the form of hardware (products and processes) and software (formulae and simulation) provide a limitless range of strategic options and are almost infallible. However, even the most advanced weapons can fail to deliver what they promise; they are notoriously unreliable; they are susceptible to neutralization by counter-measures and their effectiveness over time declines dramatically. Vietnam was in many respects a business systems war where the massive technological edge in firepower and air mobility, coupled with sophisticated strategic evaluation and planning, deluded the US into thinking that it could win an unconventional war using conventional strategies which emphasized making do with less infantry on the ground. Without continuous physical ground superiority the US was never able to fully counter the unconventional tactics of the Viet-Cong and North Vietnamese and never attained a decisive military victory. The British aerospace companies pioneered civil turbo-prop and jet airliners and engines in the late 1940s, well ahead of their US and French competitors but deluded themselves by assuming that their proven technological prowess sold products more effectively than highly trained salesmen. From fourteen major airframe and five major aero-engine manufacturers in 1950, competition had forced such mergers and withdrawals from the industry that by 1983 there were only two major airframe and one major aero-engine manufacturers left in the UK.

In war and business the function of technology has been to prevent close quarter còmbat as both generals and executives share the same reluctance to 'mix it' in close combat. Paradoxically, technology limits the intensity of combat while military and business history demonstrate time and again that generals and executives who are prepared to slug it out toe-to-toe with the enemy, have a far greater chance of winning the engagement. The British, in the battle for Goose Green in the Falklands War, frontally attacked and defeated a well entrenched Argentine force outnumbering the British by almost 4 to 1. While the opposing forces were evenly matched in weaponry the fierce determination and resolve of the British, who kept on attacking, finally broke the commitment of the Argentines.

IBM, a very late starter in the personal computer market in the US, faced formidable, entrenched, competition from the market originator and five year market leader, Apple, and a number of other major competitors such as Commodore, Texas Instruments, Atari and Coleco. IBM, in a massive frontal attack on the personal computer market, achieved market leadership and a 26% market share within 18 months of launch by outselling, outdistributing and outpromoting its estimated 150 rivals. IBM succeeded by being prepared and able to fight for distribution and shelf space through merchandising retailer-by-retailer, and for sales customer-by-customer through strong media promotion and an established image in the computer market.

No battle for territory or market share has yet been won by a formula, a computer or by remote control run by generals and executives buried in command bunkers isolated from the front line. Battles are won by hard fighting; by the practical hands-on experience of a general or executive able to make the intuitively right decision at the right place and time; and by the spearcarriers in the front line — the troops and people in research, manufacturing, finance, sales and service, who are better led, supplied, trained and motivated to win. In the markets of the 1980s, blind obedience to 'magic' models or a series of cookbook formulae have proved fatal to companies trying to cope with the effects of economic and social dislocation. Bottom line, sophisticated analytical techniques and simulation are useful for determining where a company is positioned, but are not much use when it comes to *generating* truly imaginative combat strategies or of effectively *implementing* winning tactics which emphasize close combat. Business strategy has become over-intellectualized, and the companies that win in the market-place do not get paralyzed by analysis or bogged down in strategic theory — they relentlessly pursue market leadership through the physical contest of resources.

The 1980s have already seen the decline of many leaders in a wide range of industries — aircraft (Lockheed), airlines (Braniff and Laker), baby-foods (Cow & Gate), cameras (Rollei), cars (BL and Chrysler), computer leasing (ITEL), consumer electronics (AEG-Telefunken and Texas Instruments), farm and construction equipment (International Harvester and Massey-Ferguson), lighters (Ronson), meat packing (Swift), retailing (Korvettes and Woolworths), trucks (Seddon and White Motor), and watches (ASUAG-SSIH). If these companies had mastered the elementary rules of combat and had learned how to fight, rather than to administer, they may have maintained their positions. However, this is only the tip of the iceberg. Despite the fact that the Gross National Product (GNP) grew by more than 3% in 1983 over 1982 in the US, UK and Japan, and these markets began to pick up after the recession, in excess of 64,000 companies went bankrupt in the three countries. That is, they were unable to compete effectively by earning enough cash to pay their bills. Significantly, in all the three countries bankruptcies in 1983 were at an all time high.

Ardant du Picq, the nineteenth century French military theorist, suggested that 'The instruments of battle are valuable only if one knows how to use them'. Simply, a company with an effective organization structure, ample resources, and a good product can only survive and win in-conflict situations if it knows where, when and how to fight competition. Companies and armies are not invincible — they are all vulnerable. Survival depends on the ability of companies and armies to compete in the market or on the battlefield and those with the greatest chance of survival are those who have mastered the basic elements of combat. The face of battle in the market–place has changed — gone are the conditions of the 1950s, 1960s and 1970s where the key managerial combat skills centred on outproducing competition and introducing new products where pent–up demand and growing consumer affluence provided almost limitless opportunities for growth. Companies in the 1980s are faced with multiple challenges to their security, sovereignty and power:

1. Many consumer and industrial markets are mature or are in decline. Under these conditions combatants have become more desperate, the fighting for share and leadership has become more intense and inevitably the corporate casualty rate has increased.

2. In high growth markets, invariably technology driven, the technology evolves so rapidly that companies are continuously faced with new competitors attracted by growth and profit opportunities and with product displacement by superior technology.

3. Competitors are more powerfully armed with technological, financial, productive and marketing capabilities than ever before, and as national and regional markets more rapidly saturate they become expansionist, which poses global threats.

4. The once predictable S-curve of the product life–cycle has shortened in length and time in response to shifting consumer

demands, and the effects of cheap and easily accessible technology which rapidly reduce specialty products to near commodities with an inevitable decline in margins.

The battlefield of the market-place has changed to reflect economic dislocation — recession and unemployment — and social change — attitudes, behaviour, and life-style shifts. Consumers are more cost-conscious and value-driven which has opened up new segments in the market, and advances in CAD/CAE/CAM techniques, robotics and flexible manufacturing systems, have reduced the differential in economies of scale between large and small manufacturers. These new segments have been exploited by small, highly aggressive companies outmanœuvring their large, high cost bureaucratic foes who cannot fight low cost competition.

In response to the new dynamics of the market, companies have largely concentrated on lowering their raw material, labour and physical resource costs, and there are now few opportunities in many companies for major gains through cost reduction. The only significant opportunity for real market improvement now comes from outmanœuvring competitors. There are no traditions in business, as there are in politics, of accommodation, compromise consensus, or detente, since they are anti-competitive. Companies faced with challenges to their security, sovereignty and power must fight for survival by outmanœuvring their competitors or face defeat. The end-game for companies in the 1980s is survival and under current market conditions the game plan for survival is conflict-orientated policies emphasizing deterrence, offence, defence, and alliance strategies which are based on proven military strategies.

Source References

1. Harvard Business Review, September-October, 1982.

2. Newsweek, July 26, 1982.

3. International Management, August, 1981.

4. Business Week, May 20, 1970 and Fortune, July 9, 1984.

5. Business Week, August 23, 1982.

6. Harvard Business Review, September-October, 1981.

7. McKinsey Quartely, Spring, 1981.

8. International Management, August, 1982.

9. Fortune, July 23, 1984.

10. The Financial Times, August 12, 1982.

11. *op. cit*. The Financial Times

12. The Economist, December 24, 1983.

13. Fortune, March 19, 1984.

14. The Wall Street Journal, April 16, 1982.

15. Fortune, August 22, 1982.

16. Fortune, July 9, 1984, and The Financial Times, December 6, 1984.

17. The Financial Times, August 12, 1982.

18. Business Week, June 22, 1981.

19. Journal of Marketing, Volume 36, 1981.

20. Fortune, January 25, 1982.

21. Harvard Business Review, September–October, 1982

22. The Financial Times, October 15, 1982.

23. Forbes, March 14, 1983.

GLOSSARY OF TERMS

Terms such as 'battles' for market share, 'fighting' brands and promotional 'campaigns' crept into business usage a long time ago and are commonly used to convey the emotional nature and emphasize the physical aspects of business conflict. Beyond this limited use of colloquialisms there is a wide spectrum of concepts and principles which translate readily from the military and political environment to business.

The following glossary covers terms which are directly relevant to both forms of conflict and expresses these concepts and principles in business terms.

active defence

> The use of a company's marketing, technological, financial and human resources to protect its market position from attack by competitors.

alliance

> The banding together of two or more companies to protect against competitive attacks or to combine resources to attack other companies.

attrition

> The gradual wearing down of a competitors' defences.

blitzkreig (lightning war)

> A swift, sudden combined offensive using shock tactics to weaken a competitors' morale, precipitate a disintegration of the defence and force a retreat from the market.

bridgehead (or beachead)

> Establishing a position in the market-place which provides a

base to attack competitors in other segments and niches in the market.

brinkmanship

Seeking advantage by creating the impression that a company is willing and able to pass the brink of war with a competitor to protect its market position rather than concede.

buffer zone

A segment of the market that physically separates two other segments each dominated by rival companies.

camouflage

The use of concealment by a company to minimize the possibility of a competitor detecting tactical actions and strategic manœuvres.

capability

The ability of a company to execute specific strategies and tactics.

chain of command

The succession of executives from chairman to supervisor through which command is exercised.

choke–point

A bottleneck created by a company such as restricting raw materials' availability which can be used to control the market.

clandestine intelligence

Business research activities conducted surreptitiously to avoid discovery by competitors.

coalition conflict

A conflict where one or more companies band together to attain or protect common business objectives.

collective security

Common actions by an association of companies to preserve the well–being of the group. Since these actions are frequently regarded as anti–competitive they are usually performed by trade associations.

command and control

The arrangement of facilities, equipment, personnel and procedures used to acquire, process and distribute data needed by management to plan, direct and control business operations.

commitment

An obligation to carry out a given corporate policy.

containment

Measures taken to discourage or prevent the expansion of a competitors' market share.

contingency plans

Preparation for major events that can be reasonably anticipated and which would have a detrimental effect on corporate security, position or power if the events occurred.

co–ordinated attack

A carefully planned and executed offence where a company's resources are employed in such a way as to utilize their strengths to the greatest advantage.

core area

The cluster of markets of great strategic importance to a company whose penetration or control by competitors would have a major profit impact on the company and could even threaten the company's long–term survival.

cost–effectiveness

A condition that matches ends (objectives) with means

(resources) in ways that create maximum advantage at minimum expense.

counterforce strategies

The concepts, plans, resources and actions used to destroy the market capabilities of a competitor and include challenges to patents, trademarks, copyright and advertising claims of a competitor, and the introduction of rival products.

counter-insurgency

Activities designed to destroy the effectiveness of competitive intelligence gathering activities and to protect a company from subversion.

covert intelligence

Business research conducted in such a way that competitors are unable to identify the sponsoring company.

credibility

Clear evidence that capabilities and corporate will are sufficient to support the expressed business policies of a company.

crisis management

Emergency actions taken by management to control or terminate activities which would jeopardize or seriously affect a company's business interests.

critical terrain

A single market of great strategic importance to a company where the seizure or control of that market by a competitor would have a major impact on the company's viability.

cumulative strategies

A collection of seemingly random but planned actions which, over time, create crushing results on competitors.

damage limitation

Active and passive efforts taken by a company to restrict the level of devastation caused by competitive attacks on the firm's market position.

D–day

The day on which an attack is launched on a competitor or group of competitors.

deception

Actions taken by companies to conceal their plans and the real intention of their actions from competitors.

defeat

Failure to attain stated business objectives as a result of competitive intervention or a failure to protect market share in the face of competitive attacks.

defence

Protective measures taken by a company designed to resist physical and psychological attacks on its market share.

defence in depth

Protective measures using successive positions along the line of a competitive attack, as opposed to a single point of resistance, which are designed to absorb, and progressively weaken, competitive penetration in preparation for a counter-offence.

deployment

The physical positioning of a company's resources to support its business objectives.

deterrence

Measures to prevent, rather than prosecute, conflict in the market, using psychological as opposed to physical means to dissuade competitive aggression.

direct strategies

> Offensive and defensive business strategies in which the use of physical pressure, as opposed to psychological deterrence, predominates.

division

> The standand, fully or partially self-contained, business unit, organized along product or geographical lines, which is able to operate semi-autonomously from the rest of the corporation and which pursues specific business objectives related to its product or market responsibilities.

economy of force

> The principles on which an executive uses the right mix and quality of resources to achieve objectives with the minimum losses or wasted effort.

envelopment

> The complete encirclement of a competitor by developing a range of products and services to compete directly with the competitor in all the segments of the market occupied by that competitor.

escalation

> An increase in the scope or intensity of a conflict between companies.

firebreak

> A psychological barrier inhibiting escalation from one level of conflict to another, as from national to international competition.

firepower

> The amount of resources that a company can direct at a competitor.

first strike

> The initial offensive move which may provide the opportunity for a company to eliminate competitive retaliation.

flank attack

> Assaults on competitors where a company uses geography, market conditions or product differentiation to separate the market into smaller and more manageable segments to make competitors more vulnerable to a concerted attack.

flank positioning

> The defensive repositioning of products, services or of company resources, to meet expected competitive thrusts.

flexible response

> The capability of a company to act effectively against a competitive attack across the spectrum of market conflict at times, places and in manners, of the defenders choosing.

force

> The use of physical coercion, as opposed to psychological pressure, against a competitor to attain a company's business objectives.

frontal attack

> The direct assault on a competitors market position.

front line

> The line of contact, for example, retail shelf space, in the market between two opposing companies.

graduated response

> The incremental use of a company's resources to accommodate a competitors escalation in a conflict.

grand stategy

Corporate strategy — The art and science of employing a company's resources to exert desired types and degrees of control over competition by applying force, the threat of force, indirect pressures, diplomacy and subterfuge, to attain corporate objectives.

guerrilla warfare

An extreme form of unconventional offence using primarily illegal methods such as pirating copyright, patents and trademarks to achieve market share objectives.

hard target

A market share protected against competitive attacks by an array of position defences.

indirect strategy

Any business strategy that emphasizes political, economic, social and psychological pressures against competitors rather than force.

information

Unprocessed data that can be converted into business intelligence.

infrastructure

The basic facilities, equipment, services and organization structure of a company *or* the underlying economic, financial, distributive, customer and competitive systems and government policies affecting a market.

insurance

The prudent use of a company's reserves to hedge against inaccurate estimates of the situation, competitive technological surprise and unforeseen environmental changes in the market.

intelligence

> The product arising from the collection, evaluation, analysis, integration and interpretation of business information.

intention

> A company's aim to carry out a specific course of action.

internal security

> The state of law and order prevailing within a company.

isolation strategy

> Plans and operations designed to by-pass a competitor's strongly defended products and services to attack more vulnerable targets.

kamikazi (divine wind) attack

> An attack on a competitor inflicting limited damage which will not be survivable by the attacker.

launch-on-warning

> Retaliatory strikes triggered on notification that a competitive attack is in progress, but before that attack violates the defenders market position.

lebensraum (living space)

> International business development policies — the additional market territory deemed necessary to sustain a company's economic well-being.

lines of communication

> The essential routes used by a company to move personnel, information and products and services within the company and in the market-place.

logistics

> A company's plans and operations involving the design,

development, acquisition, storage, movement, distribution, maintenance, evacuation and disposition of material; the movement, deployment and benefits of personnel; the acquisition or construction, maintenance, disposition and operation of facilities; and the acquisition or furnishing of services.

manœuvre

A calculated movement of a company's resources to fulfil the requirements of offensive and defensive strategies.

massive retaliation

Countering competitive aggression of any type using all the power of the company's resources to defeat an attack on its market position.

mobile defence

The ability to shift personnel, equipment and supplies effectively and efficiently to meet competitive threats and attacks.

mobilization

The act of preparing for market conflict by assembling and organizing raw materials, productive, financial and marketing resources: focusing all assets to meet corporate business objectives and readying the functions for market conflict.

morale

The state of mind of employees which measures the will to win. High morale is essential to attain business objectives, low-morale will ensure defeat in the market.

objectives

The fundamental aims, goals or purposes of a company toward which policies are directed and power applied.

offence

Measures taken by a company to attack a competitor with the aim of capturing all or part of its rivals' market share.

l'offence a l'outrance (blind attack at all costs)

Vigorous all-out attack on a competitor where the costs of the attack are discounted in the interests of achieving market share but which bleed the resources of both the attacker and the defender.

overkill

Resources applied in excess of that which should be adequate to attain specific business objectives.

overt intelligence

Business research conducted openly where the sponsoring company can be identified.

parity

Where opposing companies possess resource capabilities that are approximately equal in overall quality, quantity and effectiveness.

passive defence

All actions taken, other than force, to minimize the effects of competitive aggression. These include the use of mobility and subterfuge.

peace

A rare condition characterized by the absence of aggression between companies in the market.

penetration

An offensive manœuvre which attempts to break through a competitor's defences, widen the gap created and destroy the competitor's market position.

piecemeal attacks

The use of a company's resources, one element at a time, in an attack on a competitor.

position defence

The protection of a company's position and its particular niches or segments in the market rather than the defence of the overall market.

policies

Statements of guidance adopted by companies in the pursuit of business objectives.

political warfare

The offensive or defensive use of diplomacy, negotiation and propaganda to achieve business' objectives by manipulating and accommodating the key groups — competitors, customers, suppliers and government agencies — who influence the market–place.

power

The sum total of any company's capabilities or potential derived from its available productive, financial, technological and human resources and its inherent skills which are unified by management leadership into a cohesive form.

power politics theory of business conflict

Market conflict arising from a company's pursuit of incompatible goals involving the security, market power and prestige of other companies in the market; the company is a unique sovereign unit and there is a lack of truly enforceable constraints on company to company behaviour in the market–place.

pre–emptive strike

An attack on a competitor initiated on the basis of incontrovertible evidence that a competitive attack is imminent.

principle

> A governing law of corporate conduct; an opinion, attitude or belief that has a directing influence on the style and culture of a company.

principles of business warfare

> The collection of historical operating facts distilled from market experience used by strategists to select suitable courses of actions to achieve business objectives.

production base

> The total productive capacity that a company can make available to satisfy foreseeable competitive needs, together with the plans and programmes needed to put those productive resources to effective use.

propaganda

> Any form of communication designed to influence the opinions, emotions, attitudes or behaviour of competitors, customers, suppliers and government agencies to support the company's objectives.

psychological warfare

> The planned use of propaganda to influence competitors' behaviour in ways that further the company's business objectives.

pyrrhic victory

> Securing a company's business objectives, despite competitive intervention, at a resource cost so high in proportion to the gains that the victory provides a limited competitive gain for the company.

realpolitik (realistic politics)

> Market development policies. An expansionist company policy with the sole principle of advancing the company's business interests.

reconnaissance

> Actions designed to detect intelligence about the activities and resources of a competitor.

risk

> The danger of disadvantage or defeat that results from a gap between the ends (objectives) and means (resources) of a company.

scorched-earth policy

> The devastation of a market, for example by reducing prices to below costs, to leave nothing salvageable to a competitor.

second front

> The introduction of a second product or product line (a 'fighting brand') into the market to create additional resource pressures on a competitor and to deflect that competitor's pressures on the company's major product line.

second stike capability

> The ability of a company to survive a first competitive surprise strike and retaliate effectively against that competitor.

security

> The protection of a company from all types of external aggression including industrial espionage, covert competitive intelligence and annoyance.

sequential strategy

> A series of discrete, interrelated steps that are carefully planned in terms of anticipated business results.

show of force

> The purposeful exhibition of a company's resources to a competitor or potential competitor to reinforce the company's deterrent demands.

soft target

> A market share which is lightly held or unprotected by a competitor's defences.

strategic centre of gravity

> The key managerial decision point of a company.

strategic plans

> Short-, medium- and long-term plans to deploy a company's resources to meet defined business objectives.

strategic reserve

> Uncommitted resources of a company which can be used to support corporate objectives, as and when required.

strategy

> The organized *deployment* of a company's resources to achieve specific business objectives against competition from rival firms.

subversion

> Actions designed to undermine the competitive strengths of an adversary such as executive raiding and patent and trademark contests.

sufficiency

> The sum of the quality and quantity of a company's resources adequate to achieve its business objectives without waste.

superiority

> A situation where a company possesses markedly greater quantity and quality of resources than its competitors.

survivability

> The ability of a company to withstand a major competitive attack and still function effectively.

tactics

The detailed methods used to carry out strategic plans which involve the *employment* of a company's resources to win battles in the market-place.

talionic attack

An eye-for-an-eye exchange where the punishment inflicted by a company corresponds in degree to the damage to its business received from a competitor.

target

The competitors market position or share to be seized or controlled by a company.

technological warfare

The offensive and defensive use of R&D involving products and production processes which are designed to meet company objectives by augmenting its competitive advantage or neutralizing a competitors R&D capabilities.

threat

The capabilities, intentions and actions of competitors to prevent or interfere with the successful fulfilment of a company's objectives.

throw-weight

The amount of a company's resources used to achieve a specific objective.

total war

A conflict in which the productive, financial, R&D, marketing and human resources of one company are fully committed and the survival of that company is at stake.

trojan horse strategy

A strategic manœuvre designed to gain entrance to the market without provoking an immediate competitive response through subterfuge by hiding the true objectives of a company.

unconventional offence

Activities supporting conventional offence which emphasize unconventional methods including legal manœuvres designed to weaken a competitor's ability to defend its market position.

victory

The attainment of a company's business objectives despite competitive activity, without suffering critical damage to the company's resources.

vulnerability

The susceptibility of a company to any competitive action which would diminish the company's capabilities or damage the company's security.

war

A condition characterized by hostile activities or intent in the relations between two or more companies which occur as a result of a miscalculation by management or the over concentration of power and profits in the market-place which encourage competitive attack.

weaponry

Technological, productive, marketing and financial tools and techniques used by a company to obtain a competitive advantage over an adversary.

wild card theory

A term used to characterize an unpredictable event which is likely to have far-reaching effects on the business if it should occur.

withdrawal

The disengagement and retreat from a market due to product failure or adverse technological, social or economic conditions which have made the company's position untenable.

BIBLIOGRAPHY

Business

A.D. Chandler, *Strategy and Structure*, MIT Press, Cambridge, 1963.

K.K. Cox & V.J. McGinnis, *Strategic Market Decisions*, Prentice–Hall, Englewood Cliffs, 1982.

D.W. Cravens, *Strategic Marketing, Irwin*, Homewood, 1982.

J.H. Davidson, *Offensive Marketing*, Cassell, London, 1972.

P.F. Drucker, *The Age of Discontinuity*, Pan Piper, London, 1971.

R.F. Hartley, *Marketing Mistakes*, Grid Publishing, Columbus, 1981.

R. Heller, *The Business of Success*. Sidgwick & Jackson, London, 1982.

B.D. Henderson, *Henderson on Corporate Strategy*, ABT Books, Cambridge, 1979.

R.A. Kerin & R.A. Peterson, *Perspectives on Strategic Marketing Management*, Allyn & Bacon, Boston, 1980.

T. Levitt, *Innovation in Marketing*, Pan, London, 1962.

I.C. McMillan, *Strategy Formulation — Political Concepts*, West Publishing, St. Paul, 1978.

K. Ohmae, *The Mind of the Strategist*, McGraw–Hill, 1982.

T.J. Peters & R.H. Watermann, *In Search of Excellence*, Harper & Row, New York, 1981.

M.E. Porter, *Competitive Strategy*, The Free Press, New York, 1980.

D. Ricks, *Big Business Blunders — Mistakes in Multinational Marketing*, Dow Jonesrwin, Homewood, 1983.

W.E. Rothschild, *Strategic Alternatives*, Amacom, New York, 1979.

B. Taylor & D. Hussey, Eds., *The Realities of Planning*, Pergamon Press, Oxford, 1982.

Warfare

M.H. Carver, *War Since 1945*, Putnam, New York, 1981.

D.G. Chandler, *Atlas of Military Strategy*, Arms and Armour Press London, 1980.

J.M. Collins, *Grand Strategy: Principles and Practices*, Naval Institute Press, Annapolis, 1973.

C. Cook & J. Stevenson, *The Atlas of Modern Warfare*, Putnam, New York, 1978.

M. Van Creveld, *Supplying War*, Cambridge University Press, New York, 1977.

J.F.C. Fuller, *The Decisive Battles of the Western World*, Vols. 1 & 2, Granada, London, 1981.

P. Griffith, *Forward Into Battle*, Anthony Bird, London, 1981.

J.D. Hittle, *Jomini and his Summary of the Art of War*, Military Service Publishing, Harrisburg, 1947.

M. Howard, *The Causes of Wars*, Unwin, London, 1983.

J. Keegan, *The Face of Battle*, Cape, London, 1976.

B. Liddell Hart,
    History of the First World War, Pan, London, 1972.
    History of the Second World War, Pan, London, 1972.
    Strategy, The Indirect Approach, Faber, London, 1954.
    The Sword and the Pen, (Ed. A. Liddell Hart), Crowell, New York, 1976.

B.L. Montgomery, *A History of Warfare*, World Publishing, Cleveland, 1968.

R. Parkinson, *The Encyclopedia of Modern War*, Stein & Day, New York, 1977.

C.M. Providence, Ed., *The Patton Principles*, Providence Publishing, San Diego, 1979.

A. Rapoport, Ed., *Clausewitz on War*, Penguin, London, 1968.

H.G. Summers, *On Strategy: A critical analysis of the Vietnam War*, Presidio Press, Novato, 1982.

Sun Tzu, (Ed., J. Clavell), *The Art of War*, Hodder & Stoughton, London, 1981.

INDEX

MORE ABOUT PENGUINS, PELICANS, PEREGRINES AND PUFFINS

For further information about books available from Penguins please write to Dept EP, Penguin Books Ltd, Harmondsworth, Middlesex UB7 0DA.

In the U.S.A.: For a complete list of books available from Penguins in the United States write to Dept DG, Penguin Books, 299 Murray Hill Parkway, East Rutherford, New Jersey 07073.

In Canada: For a complete list of books available from Penguins in Canada write to Penguin Books Canada Ltd, 2801 John Street, Markham, Ontario L3R 1B4.

In Australia: For a complete list of books available from Penguins in Australia write to the Marketing Department, Penguin Books Australia Ltd, P.O. Box 257, Ringwood, Victoria 3134.

In New Zealand: For a complete list of books available from Penguins in New Zealand write to the Marketing Department, Penguin Books (N.Z.) Ltd, Private Bag, Takapuna, Auckland 9.

In India: For a complete list of books available from Penguins in India write to Penguin Overseas Ltd, 706 Eros Apartments, 56 Nehru Place, New Delhi 110019.

THE PENGUIN ENGLISH DICTIONARY

The Penguin English Dictionary has been created specially for today's needs. It features:

* More entries than any other popularly priced dictionary
* Exceptionally clear and precise definitions
* For the first time in an equivalent dictionary, the internationally recognised IPA pronunciation system
* Emphasis on contemporary usage
* Extended coverage of both the spoken and the written word
* Scientific tables
* Technical words
* Informal and colloquial expressions
* Vocabulary most widely used *wherever* English is spoken
* Most commonly used abbreviations

It is twenty years since the publication of the last English dictionary by Penguin and the compilation of this entirely new *Penguin English Dictionary* is the result of a special collaboration between Longman, one of the world's leading dictionary publishers, and Penguin Books. The material is based entirely on the database of the acclaimed *Longman Dictionary of the English Language*.

1008 pages   051.139 3   £2.50   ☐

PENGUIN REFERENCE BOOKS

☐ *The Penguin Map of the World*   £2.50

Clear, colourful, crammed with information and fully up-to-date, this is a useful map to stick on your wall at home, at school or in the office.

☐ *The Penguin Map of Europe*   £2.95

Covers all land eastwards to the Urals, southwards to North Africa and up to Syria, Iraq and Iran * Scale = 1:5,500,000 * 4-colour artwork * Features main roads, railways, oil and gas pipelines, plus extra information including national flags, currencies and populations.

☐ *The Penguin Map of the British Isles*   £1.95

Including the Orkneys, the Shetlands, the Channel Islands and much of Normandy, this excellent map is ideal for planning routes and touring holidays, or as a study aid.

☐ *The Penguin Dictionary of Quotations*   £3.95

A treasure-trove of over 12,000 new gems and old favourites, from Aesop and Matthew Arnold to Xenophon and Zola.

☐ *The Penguin Dictionary of Art and Artists*   £3.95

Fifth Edition. 'A vast amount of information intelligently presented, carefully detailed, abreast of current thought and scholarship and easy to read' – *The Times Literary Supplement*

☐ *The Penguin Pocket Thesaurus*   £1.95

A pocket-sized version of Roget's classic, and an essential companion for all commuters, crossword addicts, students, journalists and the stuck-for-words.

A CHOICE OF PENGUINS

☐ **Small World David Lodge**   £2.50

A jet-propelled academic romance, sequel to *Changing Places*. 'A new comic débâcle on every page' – *The Times*. 'Here is everything one expects from Lodge but three times as entertaining as anything he has written before' – *Sunday Telegraph*

☐ **The Neverending Story Michael Ende**   £3.50

The international bestseller, now a major film: 'A tale of magical adventure, pursuit and delay, danger, suspense, triumph' – *The Times Literary Supplement*

☐ **The Sword of Honour Trilogy Evelyn Waugh**   £3.95

Containing *Men at Arms, Officers and Gentlemen* and *Unconditional Surrender*, the trilogy described by Cyril Connolly as 'unquestionably the finest novels to have come out of the war'.

☐ **The Honorary Consul Graham Greene**   £1.95

In a provincial Argentinian town, a group of revolutionaries kidnap the wrong man . . . 'The tension never relaxes and one reads hungrily from page to page, dreading the moment it will all end' – Auberon Waugh in the *Evening Standard*

☐ **The First Rumpole Omnibus John Mortimer**   £4.95

Containing *Rumpole of the Bailey*, *The Trials of Rumpole* and *Rumpole's Return*. 'A fruity, foxy masterpiece, defender of our wilting faith in mankind' – *Sunday Times*

☐ **Scandal A. N. Wilson**   £2.25

Sexual peccadillos, treason and blackmail are all ingredients on the boil in A. N. Wilson's new, *cordon noir* comedy. 'Drily witty, deliciously nasty' – *Sunday Telegraph*

A CHOICE OF PENGUINS

☐ *Stanley and the Women* **Kingsley Amis** £2.50

'Very good, very powerful . . . beautifully written . . . This is Amis *père* at his best' – Anthony Burgess in the *Observer*. 'Everybody should read it' – *Daily Mail*

☐ *The Mysterious Mr Ripley* **Patricia Highsmith** £4.95

Containing *The Talented Mr Ripley*, *Ripley Underground* and *Ripley's Game*. 'Patricia Highsmith is the poet of apprehension' – Graham Greene. 'The Ripley books are marvellously, insanely readable' – *The Times*

☐ *Earthly Powers* **Anthony Burgess** £4.95

'Crowded, crammed, bursting with manic erudition, garlicky puns, omnilingual jokes . . . (a novel) which meshes the real and personalized history of the twentieth century' – Martin Amis

☐ *Life & Times of Michael K* **J. M. Coetzee** £2.95

The Booker Prize-winning novel: 'It is hard to convey . . . just what Coetzee's special quality is. His writing gives off whiffs of Conrad, of Nabokov, of Golding, of the Paul Theroux of *The Mosquito Coast*. But he is none of these, he is a harsh, compelling new voice' – Victoria Glendinning

☐ *The Stories of William Trevor* £5.95

'Trevor packs into each separate five or six thousand words more richness, more laughter, more ache, more multifarious human-ness than many good writers manage to get into a whole novel' – *Punch*

☐ *The Book of Laughter and Forgetting*
Milan Kundera £3.95

'A whirling dance of a book . . . a masterpiece full of angels, terror, ostriches and love . . . No question about it. The most important novel published in Britain this year' – Salman Rushdie

A CHOICE OF PENGUINS

A CHOICE OF PENGUINS

☐ **Man and the Natural World Keith Thomas**   £4.95

Changing attitudes in England, 1500–1800. 'An encyclopedic study of man's relationship to animals and plants . . . a book to read again and again' – Paul Theroux, *Sunday Times* Books of the Year

☐ **Jean Rhys: Letters 1931–66**
  Edited by Francis Wyndham and Diana Melly   £3.95

'Eloquent and invaluable . . . her life emerges, and with it a portrait of an unexpectedly indomitable figure' – Marina Warner in the *Sunday Times*

☐ **The French Revolution Christopher Hibbert**   £4.50

'One of the best accounts of the Revolution that I know . . . Mr Hibbert is outstanding' – J. H. Plumb in the *Sunday Telegraph*

☐ **Isak Dinesen Judith Thurman**   £4.95

The acclaimed life of Karen Blixen, 'beautiful bride, disappointed wife, radiant lover, bereft and widowed woman, writer, sibyl, Scheherazade, child of Lucifer, Baroness; always a unique human being . . . an assiduously researched and finely narrated biography' – *Books & Bookmen*

☐ **The Amateur Naturalist**
  Gerald Durrell with Lee Durrell   £4.95

'Delight . . . on every page . . . packed with authoritative writing, learning without pomposity . . . it represents a real bargain' – *The Times Educational Supplement.* 'What treats are in store for the average British household' – *Daily Express*

☐ **When the Wind Blows Raymond Briggs**   £2.95

'A visual parable against nuclear war: all the more chilling for being in the form of a strip cartoon' – *Sunday Times.* 'The most eloquent anti-Bomb statement you are likely to read' – *Daily Mail*

A CHOICE OF PENGUINS

☐ *The Diary of Virginia Woolf*
Edited by Quentin Bell and Anne Olivier Bell

'As an account of the intellectual and cultural life of our century, Virginia Woolf's diaries are invaluable; as the record of one bruised and unquiet mind, they are unique' – Peter Ackroyd in the *Sunday Times*

☐ Volume One	£4.50
☐ Volume Two	£4.50
☐ Volume Three	£4.95
☐ Volume Four	£5.50
☐ Volume Five	£5.95

These books should be available at all good bookshops or newsagents, but if you live in the UK or the Republic of Ireland and have difficulty in getting to a bookshop, they can be ordered by post. Please indicate the titles required and fill in the form below.

NAME _____ BLOCK CAPITALS

ADDRESS _____

_____

_____

Enclose a cheque or postal order payable to The Penguin Bookshop to cover the total price of books ordered, plus 50p for postage. Readers in the Republic of Ireland should send £IR equivalent to the sterling prices, plus 67p for postage. Send to: The Penguin Bookshop, 54/56 Bridlesmith Gate, Nottingham, NG1 2GP.

You can also order by phoning (0602) 599295, and quoting your Barclaycard or Access number.

Every effort is made to ensure the accuracy of the price and availability of books at the time of going to press, but it is sometimes necessary to increase prices and in these circumstances retail prices may be shown on the covers of books which may differ from the prices shown in this list or elsewhere. This list is not an offer to supply any book.

This order service is only available to residents in the UK and the Republic of Ireland.

● ● ●